HOW TO
WRITE A
NOVEL
AND
PUBLISH IT ON
AMAZON

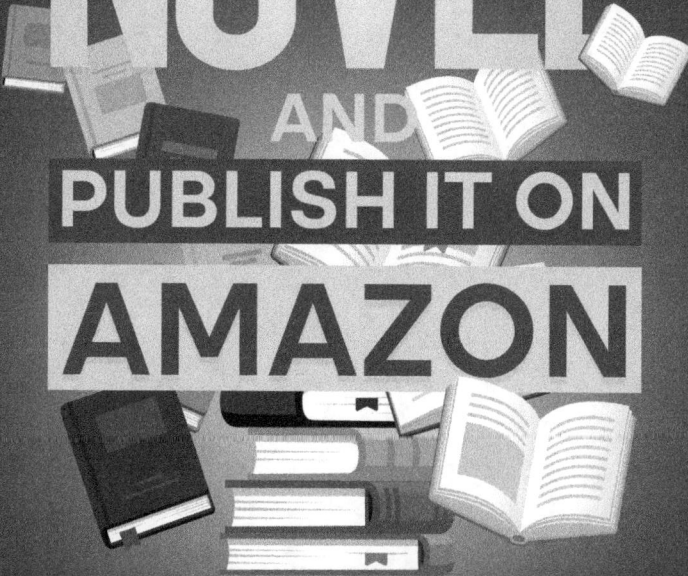

A Complete Step-By-Step Beginner's Guide to Writing
and Publishing Your First Book—at Zero Cost

JERRY MINCHEY

Contents

1. Introduction   1

2. Book Writing Magic Formula   9

3. When You Don't Have Time to Write   17

4. A Captivating Title Is Crucial   21

5. An Eye-Catching Cover   27

6. Your Unique Plot, Subplots, and Twists   33

7. Who Will Be Telling Your Story?   41

8. Describing the Setting (or Settings)   47

9. Create Interesting and Unique Characters   55

10. How to Write a Scene   63

11. How to Write Compelling Dialogue   71

12. Story Starters That Will Get You Going   77

13. How to Hook Your Readers Early   87

14. How to Structure Your Story   95

15. Write Engaging Descriptions   101

16. Conflicts are the Key   107

17. Suspense and Climax   113

18. How to End Your Book   121

19. Final Thoughts on Writing Your Novel   127

20. Rewriting, Editing, and Proofreading   131

21. Lost, Confused, or Overwhelmed? Start Here   137

22. How to Publish Your Book   141

23. How to Market Your Novel   153

24. Closing Comments   163

25. Did You Like This Book?   169

26. About the Author   171

Chapter 1

Introduction

"There are three rules for writing the novel. Unfortunately, no one knows what they are."

~ Somerset Maugham

Somerset Maugham was born in 1874 and died in 1965. A lot has been learned about writing a novel since he made that statement, but today, does anybody know what those three rules are? Let's look at the facts, and you decide.

J. K. Rowling has earned over a **billion dollars** from writing her *Harry Potter* series of books.

Here are some other authors who have earned a lot of money in the last few years from the sale of their books:

- James Patterson has earned $836 million.

- Stephen King has earned $259 million.

- Danielle Steel has earned $231 million.

- John Grisham has earned $192 million.

It's safe to say these authors know the three rules for writing a novel. And by the end of this book, you will too.

It's not only the three big rules you'll need to learn. You'll need to learn a few other little rules if you want to write a good book.

Did Mark Twain give out some bad writing advice?

He said, "Write what you know." This is the only piece of advice from Mark Twain that I disagree with. Maybe it was true back in his day when it was hard to do research on a topic, but not anymore. Today, with the help of the Internet, you can quickly become knowledgeable about almost any topic.

I would change Mark Twain's advice and say you should write what interests you. You want to write a story you'll enjoy writing. When you do that, your readers will likely enjoy reading it.

Almost any story you write will require you to do some research. Don't worry about it. Do your research and keep writing. Mark Twain didn't have that option. He was stuck with writing what he knew. In his case, that wasn't a big problem because he knew a lot.

A fast-start guide

That's what you'll find in this book. I don't try to cover everything. There are many finer points and complicated things about writing a novel that I don't attempt to cover. In this book, I will reveal the simple, straightforward techniques that will have you writing your novel in a matter of days. And the book you write will be one you'll be proud to put your name on.

Writing a novel will change your life. When you hold your published book in your hand, you'll feel a sense of pride and accomplishment you've never felt before. And, of course, when the money starts rolling in, that's a whole new wonderful feeling.

The purpose of this book is to help you write your first book.

Learning how to write a novel is like learning to play a musical instrument. You can never completely master it, but you can quickly learn the basics and start writing your novel as soon as you finish reading this book.

It's not the purpose of this book to teach you everything about how to write novels. Most of the best-selling authors don't know everything. Some don't know much, but they know how to write books in their niche and follow their winning formula. And doing this makes them a lot of money.

If you stick with simplc, straightforward writing, you'll find it easy to write your story and easy for readers to follow and enjoy your book. When you start getting into flashbacks and complicated plots, that's where readers get lost and stop reading.

If you try to add flashbacks, tell the story from multiple points of view, and have a complicated plot, there's a good chance you'll fail. The readers will get lost and put your book down. They won't leave a review (and if they do, it won't be a good one), and they won't be recommending your book to their friends.

If you try to learn everything there is to know about how to write a novel and follow the advice of all the gurus, you'll get lost and never get your book written.

Follow these four simple steps, and l guarantee your book will get written and published

- **Follow the steps in Chapter 3 and come up with a captivating title.** (The title you come up with will be a working title that you can change later.)

- **Spend $10 and have a professional eBook cover designed.** (This is your working cover. You may make changes to it later.)

- **Commit to writing 1,000 words a day, five days a week.** Your job is to put words on the page. If life gets in the way, and you don't get your 1,000 words written, write longer the next day and catch up.

- **Write your story in a linear fashion (no flashbacks) and from the main character's point of view.**

Don't try to edit or critique your work while you're writing. You can return and do that after you've finished your first draft. In 30 days, you'll have written 30,000 words, which is an acceptable number of words for your first book. You may write more, but don't feel obligated to write a long book.

Shorter books are getting more popular all the time, and they sell well.

After you've written your first draft. It will probably take another 60 days to rewrite, edit, and get your beta readers to review your book. A beta reader is someone you can get to read your book and give you honest feedback. Beta readers are notoriously slow. The difference between a beta reader and a proofreader is that beta readers are not professionals, and you're not paying them. They're reading your book as a favor to you, so be patient with them. You need several beta readers.

You will still need to format your book and get the print version of your cover designed (you can't have the cover of your print version designed until after your manuscript is formatted because you don't know how many pages the book will have, so you don't know how thick to make the spine).

I've heard people say you can't learn to write. It's a skill you have to be born with. That's BS. You absolutely can learn to write.

Ernest Hemingway said, "It's none of their business that you have to learn how to write. Let them think you were born that way."

You'll feel a profound sense of accomplishment when you write your first book and hold it in your hand. It will likely be the proudest moment of your life.

By the end of this book, you'll know the three big rules of how to write a gripping story that will captivate your readers. You'll know a lot of the little rules, too.

This book will teach you how to write a best-selling novel

When you start thinking about writing your novel, you will likely have a chaotic mix of characters, plots, and settings swirling around in your head. Your job as a writer is to harness this chaos and turn it into a smooth-flowing, intriguing story your readers will enjoy.

Writers don't all write the same way. There's not just one single way to write a novel. This book contains some suggestions. If they work for you, follow them. If they don't, forget about the suggestions and go with the techniques that work for you.

When you start writing, your goal should be to get words on the page. Later, you'll come back and edit and tweak what you've written.

As Terry Pratchett said, "The first draft is just you telling yourself the story"

Stephen King said, "Write the damn story."

Writing a novel is all about storytelling. You must have a good plot, a solid story structure, interesting and intriguing characters, and, above all, tell an engaging story.

Start by reading a lot

Stephen King said, "If you don't have time to read, you don't have time to write."

You can never learn everything about writing a novel. It's a lifetime learning process. If you wait until you feel like you know everything about writing a novel, your book will never get written.

Start by reading novels by successful authors. Read books by authors you like and admire their style. Without realizing it, your writing style will start to resemble that of the authors you are reading.

Let's get started

Your main character is standing in the middle of your setting, waiting for you. He has one heck of a problem—and he desperately wants something, but some obstacles are standing in his way. Start from here and write your story.

The secret to writing a great book that sells is to write what you love. Marketing and promotion will help, but to sell a lot of books, you must first write a great book.

Writing a book is not fun or easy. It's grueling, hard work. The fun comes when you've finished writing your book, and you're holding it in your hand. That's when you experience the feeling of joy and accomplishment.

The main takeaway from this chapter: With the information in this book, you'll see how to quickly and easily write a sizzling first draft. After that, you'll learn how to rewrite, tweak, and edit your story to end up with a great novel you'll be proud to put your name on. It will be a book readers will be talking about for years to come. Read the rest of this book, and you'll soon be writing a novel that readers will remember and tell their friends about.

Note:

As you read this book, you may notice that I have repeated some statements. I did it intentionally because I want each chapter to stand alone. With some statements repeated in different chapters, when you go back and reread a chapter, you'll have all the information on that topic at your fingertips.

Chapter 2

Book Writing Magic Formula

"I only write when inspiration strikes. Fortunately, it strikes at nine every morning."

~ William Faulkner

There are many reasons why a book doesn't sell, but the biggest reason is that it never got written.

Beginning and experienced writers alike have trouble writing. The famous writer Joseph Heller said, "Every writer I know has trouble writing." So, if you're having trouble thinking of something to say when you sit down to write, you're not alone.

Conventional wisdom doesn't work for writing a novel

The advice I'll give you in this book will go against conventional wisdom in many situations. I'll also reveal the one secret that will guarantee you that the book you start writing will be finished and published quickly. I've never seen it fail. I'll also show you non-conventional writing techniques that will keep the words flowing so you never have to experience or worry about so-called writer's block.

I call the techniques I reveal in this book my **book-writing magic formula** because it works like magic to get your book written and published.

The steps I describe in this chapter provide an overview of what I'll be teaching you later in the book. Don't try to do the things I talk about in this chapter until after you read the chapter I reference that explains how to do what I'm discussing.

In addition to getting your book written and published, I'm sure you would also like to sell a bunch of copies and make a lot of money. In Chapter 23, I'll show you how to do that and how to keep your book selling well for years to come.

Many books are still selling well 20 years after they were first published. What's their secret? I'll reveal that secret in Chapter 23.

It doesn't take any longer or more effort to write a book that will sell well and continue to sell well for years to come than to write a book that doesn't get any attention, and no one wants to read.

Personal recommendations—that's the key to selling novels

People find nonfiction books by searching Amazon for keyword phrases that describe the problem they want to solve, but they buy novels to be entertained and find them in a different way. The most common way people decide which novel to buy next is by listening to a friend's recommendation or reading an article or blog by someone they trust who recommends the book.

Another thing they count as recommendations is the number of four- and five-star reviews a book has received. A five-star review is considered a strong recommendation from someone who has read the book. Getting people to recommend your novel to their friends is the key to selling your book over the long term.

So, how do you get people to recommend your book to their friends?

Here's the formula for getting people to recommend your book

There are five important things to get readers to recommend your book to their friends.

1. **Readers have to like your book.** No one will recommend a book to their friends if they don't love it and think they will love it, too.

2. **Your book must have a title readers can remember.** How is anyone going to recommend your book if they can't remember the title?

3. **The title has to be one that readers can spell and pronounce.**

4. **It must have a memorable ending they will remember and discuss for weeks or months.**

5. **Pick out the one person you're writing your book for, and**

keep that person in mind as you write.

Without these five things going for your book, few readers will recommend it to their friends, and if readers are not recommending your book to their friends, you've lost the most important part of what drives the popularity and sales of novels.

Five simple steps to writing your novel

The first (and easiest) thing you need to decide when you're ready to start writing your novel is where your story will take place. Decide on a location (or setting, as writers call it), and you will be well on your way to writing your story.

When we get to Chapter 8, I'll explain how to choose your setting in more detail. It's easy and fun.

Looking back at the movies *South Pacific*, the famous TV series *Hawaii Five-O*, *CSI Miami*, *CSI New Orleans*, etc., you can see that the settings are necessary to the stories. The same is true with the story of Huck Finn floating down the Mississippi River.

Having your story (or at least part of it) take place in a well-known place will make your writing easier and automatically attract readers who are interested in that area. Consider this when choosing your setting.

Your story could also take place in a nondescript fictional town in Kansas, on a farm in Kentucky, or in a galaxy far, far away. Describe it properly, and you can make any place interesting—just like Tom Sawyer made the work of whitewashing a fence seem fun.

When you select your location (or locations if your story will take place in more than one place), you have made big progress and are well on your way to writing your novel.

The second thing you need to do is decide who your main character is. I'll help you do this when we get to Chapter 9, but if you've spent much time thinking about writing your novel, you probably already have some ideas about your main character. Now, it's time to settle on your hero. He may be loosely based on a real person, a combination of two or three real people, or a character you bake from scratch. You can create additional characters as your story progresses, or you may already have some ideas about the additional minor characters you want to include.

The third step is to decide who will tell the story. Writers call this the point of view or POV. I'll help you do this when we get to Chapter 7, but since you're writing your first novel, I suggest you let your main character tell the story. It will be much easier to write if you do that.

Once you have decided on your setting and main character and know who will tell the story, you need to do two more important things before you start writing.

The fourth thing you need is a general idea about the plot and genre. At the beginning of your story, the main character needs to want something (or want something to happen), and of course, some people and situations will be standing in his way of getting what he wants. These are the obstacles he will have to deal with.

You will also need to choose a genre. Is your genre Romance, Crime, Western, etc.? This is important to attract your target audience.

The fifth thing you need to do is select a reader. It needs to be a real person who you know likes the genre you picked in step four. It's important to always write for your one selected reader. Don't try to write for everybody.

When you complete these five steps (and they're easy), you'll have accomplished more than many writers have done who have been "working" on their novels for years.

Now, you're ready to start writing your book. With the previous steps taken care of, you will find that the rest of your story will move along rapidly and steadily. Let's continue. Here's what you'll do next.

Plot and structure

These are the building blocks of all great stories.

In Chapter 1, you'll introduce your hero or main character, explaining who they are, what they want, and what obstacles stand in the way of them getting what they want. You want to accomplish this in the first chapter, but don't do a massive information dump. If you do, your reader will get bored and put your book down.

The secret is to give readers only the information they need now and provide it in the dialogue as the story moves along as much as possible. Keep the narration to a minimum.

Most new writers think they need to create an outline and be linear thinkers to write a novel, but many of the best (and highest-earning authors) don't do it this way. They say trying to write with an outline stifles their creativity. They write their stories by the seat of their pants and let the characters decide what happens next.

For example, famous writers Stephen King and Margaret Atwood never use an outline when they write. They say they often don't know what will happen on the next page when writing.

But John Grisham says he never starts writing a book until he knows how it's going to end. He also writes a two or three-sentence outline of each chapter before he starts writing and changes it throughout the writing process.

Another technique that many writers use is to write a one-page synopsis of their novel rather than a detailed formal outline. This helps to keep them on track.

Obviously, all three techniques work. Go with what works for you.

The easiest way to start writing is to lct your imagination roam free—write by the seat of your pants and see how this works for you. Let your main character guide your story. It's his story. You're just writing about what he does, says, and thinks—and what happens to him. You may have a vague idea of where you think the story is going. That's fine, but don't be surprised if your story takes off in a different direction you never saw coming.

If you need to create a rough outline of a challenging chapter or section, create one and work from it. Maybe you'll find that you can write better when you're working from an outline, but don't start your writing thinking that's the only way to write a novel.

Do whatever works for you, but seriously consider starting to write your novel without an outline and see how this technique works for you.

After you finish reading this book, come back and follow the steps described in this chapter, start writing your novel, and see what happens.

The main takeaway from this chapter: Follow the formula and steps recommended in this chapter, and your book will get written and published. The best part is that it will also be a book that readers will talk about and recommend to their friends. When this happens, you will have a book that will be a best-seller and continue to sell for years.

Chapter 3

When You Don't Have Time to Write

"If it sounds like writing, rewrite it."

~ Elmore Leonard

Many people say they plan to write a book someday when they have time.

If you wish you had time to write a book but don't know how to find the time, here's something to think about.

You don't *find* time to write—you *make* time to write.

Look at everything you do daily and consider whether these things are more important than writing your book. If you can't find some things to change to a lower priority so writing your book can move up the list, it's evident that writing your book is not important to you and will not happen. It's that simple.

Is the time you spend watching TV, texting, hanging out with friends, surfing the Internet, or posting comments on Facebook more important than writing your book? You have to decide. You can either keep doing these things or write your book.

To come up with the time to write, you must assign writing a higher priority in your life than some other things you're doing.

J.K. Rowling had kids and a job, but she was able to carve out time to write the first book in her Harry Potter series. After that, she was able to quit her job and continue writing.

What activities will you give up to write a book?

All your time is already spent doing something, so if you want to write a book, you'll have to give up some things. Writing time is not going to fall out of the sky. You don't have to give up these things forever. You have to give them up until you finish writing your book.

Most likely, the three activities you could give up (or cut way back on) that would free a lot of time are watching TV, talking (and texting) with your friends, and surfing the Internet.

How about getting up an hour earlier

Many people find early mornings to be their most creative and productive time. You don't have to lose an hour of sleep to do this. All you have to do is go to bed an hour earlier.

Maybe you think you can't adjust your sleep schedule to do that, but it doesn't take you long to adapt to the new schedule when daylight savings time rolls around every year. When you set your clocks ahead one hour, you get up an hour earlier. Resetting your clocks is a way to play a trick on your brain.

Eliminate distractions

You can be much more productive when you can get away from distractions. I'm spending six months in Costa Rica this year, and it's so much easier for me to be productive here.

Most famous writers carve out a special place they can go to write. Maybe it's a room over the garage or in the attic, but, for sure, it has to be away from distractions.

Can you find a way to do this? Another way to have alone time is to close the door to the room you use as your office and put a "Do not disturb" sign on it. To make this work, you must convince your family to take your request for alone time seriously.

If there are outside noises you can't block out, how about investing in some noise-canceling headphones? You'll find that most of the ones on the market today are effective.

You need a writing routine

You won't get much done if you plan to write when you have time. To be productive, you have to stick to a routine. You don't have to follow this schedule for the rest of your life, but you'll need to do it until you finish writing your book.

Ernest Hemingway was unavailable every day until noon. He socialized all afternoon and evening but was always back at his desk writing until noon the following day.

Setting a deadline will help make things happen

You may never finish your book if you write only when you have time. But if you say, "I'll have the first draft finished in two months," or "I'll write three thousand words a week," there's a good chance you'll do whatever it takes to meet your goal. And if you don't meet your goal for some reason, you'll still be a lot closer to it than if you didn't set a goal.

The main takeaway from this chapter: Regardless of what's going on in your life, you'll find time to write if it's important to you. And if it's unimportant to you, I'm sure you'll find a good excuse for being too busy to write. If you don't write your book, accept the fact that the reason was that it wasn't important to you. Don't kid yourself and say you didn't write it because you "didn't have time."

Chapter 4

A Captivating Title Is Crucial

"Honesty is the first chapter in the book of wisdom."

~ Thomas Jefferson

Here's the question all writers struggle with:

How to come up with a title for your book?

There are several ways to come up with a great title. Ideally, create a list of a dozen or more titles and let the list marinate for a week or so before choosing.

Conventional wisdom is often wrong about many things, and a book title is one of them. Contrary to what many writers and gurus recommend, don't wait until after you finish writing your book before you give it a title. After you've given your book a working title, feel free to modify or completely change it as more ideas come to mind while you're writing your book.

Three things are essential when selecting the title of your novel

One of the best ways to launch your book and increase sales is to get readers talking about it. If you can get people to start telling their friends about your book, you'll have a best-selling book. It's that simple. The title of your book plays a vital role in making that happen. We talked about this in Chapter 2, but let's review the topic and dive deeper into it.

Here are the three things that will make or break your title.

Your book needs a title that is:

Easy to remember—People can't recommend your book if they can't remember the title.

Easy to spell—Potential readers can't send emails to their friends recommending your book if they can't spell the title, and they can't look the book up on Amazon if they can't spell the title.

Easy to pronounce—Word of mouth is a great way to promote your new book, but if your title is difficult to pronounce, people won't talk about or recommend it.

Since many readers will search for a novel someone has recommended, having a title that's easy to remember, spell, and pronounce is important. It doesn't do you any good to have someone recommend your book if the person they're recommending it to can't remember the title or how to spell it because they will never be able to search and find it on Amazon.

Don't overlook any of these three critical points. For example, don't spell a word in your title in a unique way to have a cute title. That could spell disaster for your book sales.

Here are some places you can pull titles from:

1. Pull your title from a phrase in the book.

2. Pull it from one of the scenes in the book.

3. Use the name of one of the characters.

4. Include keywords common in your genre. Certain words are common in different genres. For example, what topic would come to mind if the word "stagecoach" were in the title? What about the words taxi, prom, wedding, date, ghost, or alien? Make a list of the most common words in your genre, and consider using one in your title.

5. One of the best ways to develop a title is to let your subconscious work on the problem. Sometimes, a great title will pop into your head. You know your topic and characters well, so your subconscious mind has a lot of information to work with. Be open to the titles that pop into your head, and add them to your list for consideration.

A few more comments about titles

The title of a novel should not try to tell what the book is about or describe it in any way. The title of most novels usually doesn't mean anything or make any sense until after someone has read the book. Sometimes, they will discover the title's origin while reading the book. This is usually an enjoyable "aha" moment and a pleasant surprise for them.

Think about the following two book titles

If you have not read the book or seen the movie, you might easily think *Gone with the Wind* is a story about a sailing adventure instead of a book about the Civil War.

The title of Harper Lee's classic novel, *To Kill a Mockingbird*, tells you nothing about the book's subject, but it checks all the boxes. It's easy to remember, easy to pronounce, and easy to spell.

That title comes from a conversation in the book between Atticus and Scott, in which Atticus states that "It's a sin to kill a mockingbird" because mockingbirds simply sing their song and never harm anyone. This is an example of pulling the title from an important phrase in the book. It means something to the reader after they've read the book, but not before.

It's fun for the reader to be reading a book and stumble across the source of the title.

Four things you should never do when choosing a title for your book:

#1. Don't choose the title of an existing book or movie. It may not be illegal, but it makes finding your book harder. So, when you come up with a title you want to use, search Amazon to ensure there are no other books with that same title. Also, search Google. Maybe there's no book with that title, but is there a movie, report, organization, or something else using those words?

#2. Don't use an exclamation point in your title—and heaven help you if you use two or three. If you do, it will scream, "amateur." As a general rule, use little or no punctuation in your title. It's okay to use an apostrophe to show ownership. And for sure, don't use a period at the end of your title, even if it is a complete sentence.

#3. Never use a one-word title for your book. If someone recommends your book to a friend and they go to Amazon to find it, even though the one-word title is easy to remember, if they search Amazon for one word, they'll likely never find your book. I like short titles, but you'll need at least two or three words in your title. I like to have a title with seven words or fewer, but I sometimes exceed this number.

#4. Don't overthink selecting your title. Of course, you want to put a lot of effort and thought into coming up with the title of your novel, but don't let it consume you or get you stressed out. Coming up with the title of your book should be an enjoyable process, not a stressful endeavor.

When making your final title selection, it's okay to ask some people (who would likely be your target readers) to review the list of titles you're considering and give you their thoughts and opinions. But remember, it's your baby, and it's up to you to name it.

The main takeaway from this chapter: The title of your book is super important, so don't leave it to a last-minute effort. So many beginning writers don't put any effort into what the title of their book will be until after they have finished writing the first draft, and sometimes not until they're ready to publish their book. Doing this is a big, big mistake. You need a working title before you write a lot of content for your book. Changing your title as you write your book is fine, but start with a working title.

Chapter 5
An Eye-Catching Cover

"You can't judge a book by its cover, but you can sure sell a bunch of books if you have a good one."

~ Jayce O'Neal

Now that you have a working title, it's time to think about a cover for your book. Most authors put this step off until the last minute after they've finished writing their book. That's the wrong way to do it. Go against conventional wisdom and get a working version of your cover designed before you do much writing on your book.

Book covers are designed in layers, so changing the title is easy after creating the cover. It's so easy that my designer often doesn't charge me anything when I make the changes.

More than 65% of all the books sold worldwide (both printed and eBooks) are sold by Amazon. I assume that's how you'll sell your book, so you need a cover that will grab people's attention when browsing Amazon's books and looking at the thumbnail images.

It's not easy to get a new book noticed these days because Amazon publishes more than 7,500 new books every day.

That's why it's more important than ever for your book to have an eye-catching cover.

It takes an eye-catching cover to get your book to stand out in the crowd

To get your book noticed, you need a professional-looking and attention-grabbing cover. A dull, hard-to-read cover will not do the job. If you don't have a great cover, all the effort you put into writing your book will be for nothing. No one will ever read your great story if the cover doesn't catch the readers' attention.

The sole purpose of your book cover is to get your book noticed. It's not to tell what the book is about. Amazon's detail page has your exciting and compelling description, and potential readers will be taken to this page to learn what your book is about. But your cover has to grab their attention and get them to this page.

Another reason to have your book cover designed before you do much writing is that having an eye-catching cover designed before you start writing will keep you motivated to finish your book. I've never known anyone to have a cover designed and then not finish writing and publishing their book.

You need a professional to design your book cover

Knowing how to use Photoshop doesn't mean you know how to design book covers. For as little as $10, you can hire an expert on Fiverr.com to create a cover for your eBook. (Note that eBooks don't have a back cover.)

I've designed my own book covers in the past, but I don't do it now. Designing an attention-grabbing book cover is a skill that most graphic designers lack. You want to hire someone who has experience designing book covers.

For my last half-dozen books, I've used Olivia on Fiverr.com. You can find her at OliviaProDesign.

She is in Ukraine and will design a great eBook cover for $10.

You can't design the cover for the print version until you finish writing and formatting your book. You'll need the page count to determine how thick to make the spine, so don't worry about that now.

I usually have an idea about what photo or image I want to use on my book cover, and sometimes I know what typeface and colors I want to use, but not always. I don't use an image for some of my book covers, but most novels use one or more images on the cover.

I paid Olivia $40 to design four different front covers for this book. The one I selected is unconventional, but it's attention-getting. Remember that the purpose of a book cover is to grab a potential reader's attention and get them to take a closer look at your book.

What is necessary to have a great book cover?

Below are the essential things you need to keep in mind about book covers:

- The job of your book cover is to grab readers' attention and nothing else.

- It's essential to have a professional-looking cover.

- Make the title on the thumbnail image large and easy to read.

- The cover should not try to describe your book or tell what it's about.

- Don't use fancy fonts that are hard to read.

- Consider having an eye-catching picture on your cover.

- Compare your book cover to other books in your genre. Which one would you buy?

What do you include on the back cover?

Below are some of the things you should consider including on your back cover:

- Start with an attention-getting opening headline followed by a compelling sentence to hook the reader and pull them into your book. Many people buy books and never get around to reading them, but you're not likely to get a review from anyone who buys your book and doesn't read it.

- Include an intriguing line from your book or one of your best endorsements.

- If you have a website, be sure to include the URL.

- At the bottom of the back cover, include a paragraph titled "About the Author." People like to know information about the author of the books they read. Be sure to include your picture. Doing this will help readers feel like they know you, and they will be more likely to leave a review. This section should be written in the third-person format.

- After you've written other books, you can change the back cover and show information to promote your other books. Remember that you can change the front and back cover anytime after your book has been published. The only things you can't change are the title, subtitle, or author.

How to guarantee your book will get finished

Less than 0.6% of the books people start writing ever get finished because they lose interest and are no longer motivated to keep writing. Don't let this happen to you.

Having the cover of your book posted where you'll see it daily will motivate you to finish and publish your book.

Maybe it's happened, but I have never known anyone who has had their book cover designed and didn't finish writing and publishing their book.

The main takeaway from this chapter: The old cliché that people don't judge a book by its cover is dead wrong. That's about the only way they judge a book. That's why it's so crucial that you have a professional-looking, attention-grabbing cover. Your book deserves a professional-looking cover.

Chapter 6
Your Unique Plot, Subplots, and Twists

"No tears in the writer, no tears in the reader. No surprise in the writer, no surprise in the reader."

~ Robert Frost

Your plot is what happens in the story.

There are few (if any) new plots. They are all variations of "The boy gets the girl, The good guy wins, The bad guy gets caught and is punished," etc.

When you sit down to start writing your story (if you're not working from an outline), you probably know less about what will happen in your story than you do about what will happen in your life. You probably have ideas, and you may know what you think is going to happen and how you want things to work out.

But in your novel—just like in your life, things don't always go according to plan. At least, that's what happens if you're not working from an outline—and many great writers don't use an outline when they write.

Plot twists

What is a plot twist?

A plot twist is a revelation that changes the reader's perceptions of the story or main character. It should cause the story to shift significantly from what the reader thought would happen. An oversimplified definition of a plot twist is when your reader expects one thing, and something entirely different happens.

Just as your reader thinks they have everything figured out, if you throw a plot twist into the story and shake up their world, you will keep them turning the pages. You never want your story to be predictable.

Every good story must have a plot twist—maybe more than one. Your reader will remember a great plot twist. It's why they'll talk about your book and recommend it to their friends.

An unexpected plot twist is the one thing that will make a book unique and memorable. Of course, if the reader can see the plot twist coming, it can kill the story. And don't underestimate your reader. They can be pretty clever and pick up on clues. Use this to your advantage and leave subtle clues that lead them in the wrong direction.

All good stories must have subplots.

Subplots are secondary stories that are placed within the main story. They often pull readers into the story and keep them turning the pages as much as the main plot does.

Here are some ways you can create a subplot:

- A subplot should be crucial to your story's development. It shouldn't be there if you could remove a subplot, and it wouldn't change your story.

- Subplots should tie into the main plot. You don't want a subplot that stands alone.

- Introduce a revelation about a character's lineage. For example, the readers didn't know the villain was the main character's father (or son).

- A good use of a subplot is to complicate the main storyline.

- Start brainstorming plot twists, and then discard the first ideas that come to mind. They're too obvious.

- Don't let a subplot take over the story and become the most exciting part of your story.

- Make some items or events that have been unimportant all along suddenly become extremely important.

Here are some of the things subplots should do:

- Enhance the main story

- Offer additional tension, content, and character development

- Revolve around the main and supporting characters

- Weave into and support the main plot

- Explore and reveal a minor part of the character's personality

- Provide humanizing traits of a character to help the readers feel like they know and understand him better

- Make the main character more relatable

Add depth by including one or more emotional subplots. You have to have enticing subplots to have a good story.

Patching plot holes

Every first draft will have one or more plot holes. A plot hole is what the name implies it is. It's a hole or problem in your story.

It's easy for holes to develop in your plot. Since you probably wrote your story over several weeks or months, it's hard to remember what you said in Chapter 3 while you're writing Chapter 17.

The way to find and fix plot holes is to take a break from your manuscript for a week or two. Then, come back and read it with a fresh mind. Look at the timelines, locations, and details to see if they agree. When a character does something, does it align with their typical behavior in the previous chapters? Did all of the subplots get resolved?

Factual errors can become plot holes if the story depends on them.

Here are some examples:

- A six-shot revolver can't fire nine shots.

- An old Volkswagen Beetle was having trouble. It pulled off the road with steam coming out from the front of the car. This is an example of a plot hole since that car had an air-cooled engine in the back. There's no way to have steam coming out.

- Revolvers don't eject the shell casings.

If a subplot never gets resolved, that's also a plot hole. You can't just ignore it. Go back and fix it or delete it. Don't leave it hanging unresolved.

Plot holes make readers want to put the book down and not pick it up again. They'll be thinking, "How ignorant can this writer be?" Hopefully, your beta readers will catch these kinds of screw-ups, but maybe not. They're primarily looking for grammar errors and typos.

When making minor changes to the plot to fix plot holes, you might decide to change the plot altogether.

If your story is so complicated that fixing the plot holes is difficult, consider simplifying the plot. If a plot is hard for you to follow, you know your readers will have trouble with it. A reader who gets lost in the plot will likely give up. After all, there are plenty of other books to read.

Plot twists are important to your story

Without a plot twist or two, your story's outcome is too easy to predict. Plot twists keep the reader on his toes and interested in your story.

Ways to create a plot twist:

- Kill off a seemingly important and untouchable character.

- Something that seemed unimportant turns out to be crucial.

- Have your main character team up with the enemy to accomplish something unexpected.

- Elevate a seemingly minor character.

- Have a relationship subplot (romantic or otherwise).

- The goal of any plot twist is to drop subtle clues that the reader remembers, but doesn't recognize as clues at the time. As soon as they get to the plot twist, they will say, "Oh yeah, I should have seen that coming."

Remember that all plot twists need to be logical and make sense. Don't try to pull off something totally illogical and unlikely, and try to make the reader think it happened.

YOUR UNIQUE PLOT, SUBPLOTS, AND TWISTS
39

Did you pull off a successful plot twist?

The best way to determine if you successfully crafted a plot twist is to give your finished manuscript to your beta readers. Then, after they have read it, ask them if they expected the plot twist or saw it coming.

Overused twists:

Don't fall back on these over-used twists. You can do better than this.

- It was all a dream.

- The villain turns out to be the good guy. Of course, you want the bad guy to be someone the reader doesn't expect, but don't overdo it.

- You have too many coincidences. It's better not to rely on any, but sometimes, you almost have to have a coincidence to get the story to work. If you have to have one, it's better not to have more than one in your story. Relying on coincidences is a cop-out. When you do that, it screams amateur. Coincidences are okay if they create obstacles and make the situation worse, but they should never help or resolve a problem

The main takeaway from this chapter: Of course, your characters, settings, dialogue, and conflicts are all part of what makes a great story, but your plot, subplots, and twists are the driving forces in your unique story. Without a captivating plot, subplots, and a twist or two, your story would be a flop. Keep this in mind as you write and develop your story.

Chapter 7

Who Will Be Telling Your Story?

"Get your facts first, then you can distort them as you please."

~ Mark Twain

Writers call the question of who is telling the story the story's point of view or POV. In other words, who is narrating the story?

Stories can be told in the first or third person, and you can change between these in your story. However, this makes it harder to write and can confuse the reader unless done carefully and correctly. On rare occasions, a writer pulls off the second person, but don't try it for your first novel, if ever.

If you decide to change the POV in your book, remember that you should not change the POV in a scene, and only one change per chapter would be even better. Ideally, keeping the same POV for the whole book would be better for the reader and easier for you to write.

First-Person Narration POV

One of the easiest ways to write a book is to have the main character tell their own story. This is called the first person. Make writing your novel easy by letting your main character do the talking.

An easy way to do this is to imagine your main character, who is telling the story, as your camera. You can tell only what they see, hear, and think. That way, you won't be tempted to switch and start telling the story from a different point of view.

When the story is told from the main character's point of view (POV), it has the added advantage of helping the reader feel like they know the main character. One significant advantage of writing in the first person from the main character's point of view is that it can contribute to strong character development.

Different POV Examples

Here's an example of first-person narration: "The first day, when he walked into my office, I had no way of knowing how he was going to change my life."

Since you're not trying to learn everything about writing novels but want to write your first book, forget all the options and write your story using the easy, first-person POV technique.

If you have your main character tell the story from their point of view, it will be much easier to write, and the readers won't get lost or confused.

How an airport can help you write your story

Imagine you're waiting to board your plane, and a stranger sitting next to you starts telling you a story about something that happened to him.

Initially, you don't know the person telling you the story, but as the story moves along, you get to know him, learn more about him, and start to care more about him, which will make you care more about his story.

If you keep the airport situation in mind as you begin writing your story, I think you'll find your story much easier to write.

After all, you're just sitting in the airport, listening to the main character tell you what happened. While you're hearing the voice in your head telling you the story, you're writing it down. What could be easier?

Hear the main character in your head

Even though you're creating a fictional person, you need to get to know them well, as if they were real.

If you're basing your main character loosely on someone you know, listen to them talk. Listen carefully and pick up on their tone and phrasing. Are they usually funny, sarcastic, or excited? Do they talk fast or slow? Do they ramble a lot or get to the point quickly? Do they typically speak in long sentences or short ones? Or do they even talk in complete sentences?

If listening to them in person is impossible, try calling and chatting. Long conversations are best if you both have the time. The longer you talk, the more you'll get to know the person. What they say is not important—it's how they say it. As a last resort, try recalling times you've heard them talking. Try to hear their voice in your head.

Become your character

When writing your manuscript, you want to become the character doing the narration. The more you develop the character and get to know them, the easier this will become. If you become Huck Finn on the raft floating down the Mississippi River, it will be much easier for you to tell the story. Maybe that's what Mark Twain did when he wrote the story.

In the beginning, the voice you hear in your head may sound a lot like your own, but as your character develops and the more you get into the story, the more you will become the character. If the character has an accent, you may even start to hear the accent in your head.

Your goal should be to get inside the heads of each of your characters and know how they think and act in different situations. The more you can become your character when writing your book, the better your story will be.

Since you don't have an outline, let the main character tell you the story. You never know where they may take you or what direction your story may go.

One precaution: When telling your story in the first person, try to limit the use of "I." Don't start every sentence, or even every paragraph, with the letter "I." This can get annoying to the reader. Don't worry about this when writing your first draft, or it will cramp your creativity, but be keenly aware of it while rewriting and editing. That's when you need to fix things.

An important point to keep in mind when writing in the first person

It's easy to sometimes slip into telling your story from a perspective other than the first person. One easy way to prevent this is always to remember that you are the main character. Look at it that way.

You can tell only what the main character sees, hears, and thinks. For example, he can say, "Tammy looks angry," but he can't say, "Tammy feels angry." Your main character doesn't know how Tammy feels. All he can do is speculate. He can't say, "The detective thinks I'm lying." He can't know what the detective is thinking. He can say, "The detective probably thinks I'm lying." Putting the word "probably" in the sentence solves the problem.

When you're telling the story in the first person POV, include a lot of what the character is feeling and thinking in addition to what he's saying. If the reader doesn't know what the character is feeling and thinking, it will be difficult to connect with the character.

Two final points:

#1. An interesting advantage of telling the story from the main character's point of view is that things can happen to the main character that he didn't see coming because the narrator knows only what the main character knows at any given time.

#2. Make sure your character speaks the way you would expect him to. A 90-year-old army veteran will not talk like a high school student, and a retired army sergeant won't talk like a kindergarten teacher.

The main takeaway from this chapter: You have to decide who will tell your story before you can start writing. You have several options, but writing your story in first person from the point of view of the main character will make your story come together faster, and it will be easier to write.

Chapter 8

Describing the Setting (or Settings)

"If you want to make your dreams come true, the first thing you have to do is wake up."

~ J. M. Powers

The setting you choose is integral to your story—more important than many authors realize.

You can take the same plot, with the same characters, with their same problems, and place them in a different setting, and it will be a totally different story. Is the story taking place in London, the Florida Everglades, on the Appalachian Trail, on a cruise ship, or a small farm in rural Georgia?

The setting defines the story. When you have an exciting and intriguing setting, you start with the deck stacked in your favor. You already have the readers interested in your story.

The setting is super important, but don't make the amateur mistake of starting your book by spending a lot of time describing it. Readers don't have the patience for this. They want the story and action to begin almost immediately. If you bore them, they'll likely put your book down and go read something else.

How to set a scene without describing it?

You should include the description of the scene as part of the story in the action and dialogue. This way, rather than telling the reader everything through narration, you can let him learn about the setting. This is what is called showing rather than telling.

This way, the reader won't even realize you're describing the setting. When the reader concentrates on the story's action, drama, tension, and conflict, they won't realize that the scene is being described in the dialogue. Doing this is not easy, but when you can pull it off, you will have graduated to being a great writer. Many new writers screw up in this area more than anywhere else and use too much narration describing things the reader doesn't need to know yet.

If a detail is not important enough to become part of the action, your reader doesn't need to know it—at least, not right now.

Consider all five senses when describing your setting

You don't necessarily want to describe your main character's reactions to all five senses when describing a setting—only the ones that are, or will be, important to the story. If you were the main character, what would stand out to you? What does your main character sense when they enter the house, step outside, or get into the car?

The setting (or settings) you choose for your story are crucial, but many writers do a lousy job of selecting or describing their setting. They don't put much thought into the setting, and that's a big mistake.

When the reader can't picture the main character in a unique setting, it's hard to pull them into your story and get them hooked.

Don't interrupt your story to describe the setting in a detailed, rambling narration. It's better to incorporate the description of the setting into the dialogue or narration.

Weave action into your descriptions. Don't say that there's mud or a tree root on the path. Have someone slip in the mud, fall, or trip over the tree root.

Your character could brush the curtains aside to let more light into the dark room, close the window to keep the smoke from coming in from the fire where the neighbor is burning leaves, etc.

You don't want to describe everything your character senses in every setting, but consider each of the five things listed below and decide what description will best help move your story along.

- **Sight:** Is the room dark or brightly lit? What colors stand out? What's moving—the curtains blowing in the wind, etc.?

- **Sound:** Do they hear the TV blaring, the dogs barking, the classical music playing softly in the next room, or a baby crying?

- **Smell:** Do they smell the bacon frying, the car exhaust, the sourdough bread baking, or the burnt toast?

- **Taste:** Can they almost taste the burgers on the charcoal grill outside or the tartness of a piece of hard candy someone handed them as they walked into the room?

- **Touch:** Do they feel the breeze, the house shaking as the train goes by, or the raindrops on their head when they step outside?

Use a setting to create conflict

The setting you choose can be an excellent tool for creating conflict. A character can be in conflict because of the setting or in conflict with the setting.

If a character has just moved to a new town, started a new job, and doesn't know anybody, they could be in conflict because of the setting, and if they're lost in the mountains in the snow with no food or shelter, they could be in conflict with their setting.

Your setting influences your plot

The setting can drive or control the plot. Things can happen on the beach that can't happen in NYC, or vice versa. If you're writing your story without an outline, picture your character in a different setting. Different things will happen to him, and he will have different and unique problems that he wouldn't have in a different setting.

When you choose an exciting setting, you've done a lot to hook your readers and pull them into the story. Stack the deck in your favor and have your story take place in an interesting setting. Of course, how interesting your setting is will be determined a lot by how you describe it. Almost any setting can be made interesting with the right description.

For example, watching Tom Sawyer whitewash a picket fence in Missouri doesn't sound like an interesting or exciting setting. Still, Mark Twain turned it into one of the most memorable stories ever written.

How to choose the setting for your story

Since everything has to happen somewhere, and you are free to choose any place in the universe, how do you choose a setting for your story?

Start by thinking about what comes to mind when you think about your story.

Think about what your plot needs. Does it need to be in or near a big city? Does it need to be on a farm? Will some scenes take place on a beach? Does it need to be near a major university? You need a setting that works with all the logistics of your plot.

Consider how the main character feels about the setting. Is he dead set on getting away from it, or is he so tied to it that he could never leave, even when he knows he should? Your main character has a relationship with the setting just like he does with another character. He may have conflicts with the setting just like he does with a character.

If you're writing without an outline and your plot evolves, you may have to go back and modify your plot or setting. Don't sweat it. You can add a hospital or a police station five miles from where the main character lives if the plot later requires it.

Give the characters something to do

If you choose a setting where your character has something to do as the story progresses, your story will be easier to write and more enjoyable to read.

If they're on a sailboat, driving across the country, living in a motorhome, or remodeling an old house, there will be plenty to keep them busy.

Something could happen when your characters have something to interact with or are in a situation to keep them occupied, and your story could take off in a different direction.

You'll probably need more than one setting

Just like you'll have one main character and some minor characters, you'll likely have one main setting and some minor settings. A story might be boring if everything happens in one place. Your main character could take a trip to another country, a different town, a different side of town, or even walk into a different room. But make each scene exciting and unique.

Some settings may be in your story for only a short time. For example, your main character is in a hospital room (or a police station) after an accident.

Just like you'll have a main character and some minor characters, you'll likely have your primary setting and some minor settings in your story.

Occasionally, add a small but interesting, unexpected, and surprising detail about a setting to move your story along and keep your reader involved.

The main takeaway from this chapter: Nowhere in writing is the concept of showing rather than telling more critical than when you're describing a setting. Don't start your story with a long narrative description of the setting. Start with the action and work the description of the setting into the dialogue. Your readers will quickly learn what they need to know about the setting and never realize you were describing it to them.

Chapter 9

Create Interesting and Unique Characters

"When I used to teach writing, I would tell the students to make their characters want something right away."

~ Kurt Vonnegut

Characters are what make your story come to life. Your characters are more important than your plot.

Characters are what readers care about and are attached to

If you've read a sequel to any book, you'll likely see that the author used a different setting and plot, but the main character or characters remain the same.

Your story will need a main character or hero and, most likely, a few other realistic and interesting characters. One of the most complex parts of writing a novel is coming up with a main character readers can identify with and care about.

Early in your book, you want your readers to identify with the hero and begin to cheer for him in your story. You must also let the readers know what the hero desires and dreads the most. What does he want more than anything else, and what is he most afraid of? Maybe he's concerned about a sense of impending doom or disaster.

The doom or disaster he's concerned about doesn't have to be a life or death situation. It could be something as simple as not getting a promotion or a spouse leaving.

Bring your main character to life at the beginning of a story. Do it in the first paragraph if possible, but in the first chapter, for sure. Your reader is not hooked on your story until he's hooked on the main character.

Try to blend your character's description seamlessly into the story. This is much better than stopping your story and writing a paragraph or so describing your character. If you do a good job of this, your reader will not even realize that you're describing the character.

When you can describe your characters while keeping the story moving, readers will start to know and connect with them without even knowing they're doing it.

Don't show a picture of your characters

Let your reader's imagination create pictures of the characters in their heads. Of course, you must provide a description and some information about each character, but not too much. For example, you can say she is beautiful, has short brown hair, and is in her mid-20s. You can say she likes pizza and strawberry ice cream cake and loves country music. Let your reader come up with the rest of the character's description in their mind. You don't have to use much physical description, but it does have to be early in the story before the reader paints a mental picture.

Your characters are the secret sauce for your story

Characters can turn a ho-hum novel into an intriguing story that will pull your readers into it.

Take the time to create intriguing characters your readers can identify with and want to know more about. Your story will be easier to write when you have interesting characters. Readers like to fall in love with a hero.

Is the main character someone they can identify with? Do they love him, feel sorry for him, or want to be like him? You definitely want your readers to want to know what your main character will do next and what will happen to him.

You want your main character to be someone your readers would like to spend time with. Would they want the main character to be their boyfriend, girlfriend, husband, wife, best friend, or roommate?

You want to create exciting characters. One way to do this is to make them a mixture of more than one person. Take traits of different people you know and create a character. You could do this for all your characters.

Your characters need to all be different, with different personalities, goals, and problems.

Bake a character from scratch

One way to have an exciting character is to create them totally from scratch. Come up with the characteristics you want your character to have and roll them into your main character.

Will the character you create be honest, devious, strong, weak, intelligent, silly, witty, ambitious, lazy, hard-working, athletic, good-looking, beautiful, etc.?

You'll need a character that will keep your readers engaged and involved in your story.

You need to get to know your characters well. Your writing will be easier if you have a one-page description of each character that you can occasionally refer to. On this page, include everything you know about them. You won't use everything you know about a character in your story. But when you know your characters well, you can predict their actions in any situation.

Things you need to know about your characters

Start with what you know now and add to each character's page as you learn more about them. Your characters can change as the story progresses. They can start out shy and later become more brave and outgoing. How your characters develop and change can be part of your story.

The more you know about each character, the easier it will be to write your story. It helps you know what each character would do or say in a situation. Writing your story will be easier when you instinctively know and understand your characters.

- What does your character want and fear more than anything else?

- What is standing in the way of them getting what they want?

- Do they have a spouse or a significant other? Do they have any kids?

- Provide information about your character's family.

- Do they have a job? How did they get the job? What do they do in their job? How long have they had that job? Do they want to change jobs?

- Are they retired or planning to retire soon?

- How old is your character? You don't have to tell your readers their age, but knowing their age will make writing your story easier. It will help you know how they would act in a particular situation.

- Have they been in the military? If so, what branch? What did they do while they were enlisted? Did they like it or hate it?

- What has happened in their life that they are still dealing with?

- Where do they live? How long have they lived there? Are they thinking about moving, and if so, where and why?

- Do they have a car, boat, RV, or motorcycle? If so, describe it.

- Are they still in school? Have they graduated? Are they thinking about going back to school? Where and why?

- What are they planning for the future?

- What are they afraid will happen (or not happen)?

- What have they done that they don't want anybody to find out about?

Your characters don't have to be fully developed before you start writing your story. They can grow and change, and more can be revealed about them as the story progresses. If your characters change as the story progresses, be sure to update their pages.

Name your characters

Here are some essential things to remember about the names of your characters:

It's better if your characters' names each start with a different letter. You don't want Bill, Betty, Bob, Bo, and Barbara to be your characters.

Use names that are easy to pronounce because many people will sound out the names in their heads as they read your book.

It's okay to use a nickname. A nickname can sometimes help describe a character. What comes to mind when you hear the following nicknames?

Tank, Cowboy, Cupcake, Giggles, Rambo, Shorty, Little Joe, Bad Boy, Girly, Sunshine, Champ, Wonder Woman, and Goofball are nicknames that help your readers picture the character.

The main takeaway from this chapter: Developing interesting characters your readers can like and bond with is one of the most important parts of writing a good novel. If your readers don't like your main character, they may not even finish reading your novel. Characters are that important. Put a lot of time and effort into choosing and developing your characters. Your characters are what will make your novel.

Chapter 10

How to Write a Scene

"Write your first draft with your heart. Rewrite with your head."

~ Mike Rich

A scene is a section of your novel where a character or characters engage in action or dialogue that moves the main story along. It's a mini-story within a story. It's usually not a whole chapter. A chapter can have more than one scene.

A scene usually takes place in one place and in one period of time. That's the basic rule that defines a scene.

A scene should advance the story—therefore, something should change

If the scene had been removed from the story, the ending wouldn't have been possible, or it would have been different. Every scene should affect the outcome or direction of your story. If a scene doesn't impact the story, delete it.

What makes a scene?

#1. Change: The most defining thing that describes a scene is that something changes. Some scenes will cause a subtle change, and others will cause a pivotal shift.

#2. Conflict and what's at stake: Conflict revolves around the main character's goal or what he wants. What's at stake is what he has to lose if he doesn't achieve that goal. Conflict is what is preventing him from achieving the goal. Tension happens when the reader feels that all of this is important.

#3. Structure: A scene should be structured similarly to a story. All scenes are part of the main story, but they'll have their own internal structure similar to the big story. There should be an event, some suspense that builds up to a climax, and a close. It's just like the structure of your main story.

In most cases, it's better to tell the story in a linear fashion. Writing your story becomes difficult when you use flashbacks. If you don't do it correctly, you'll lose your readers.

A good scene should advance the plot or further develop the character. It should do both when possible, but that's not always easy. A scene is an excellent way to further develop a character. In most scenes, the reader should learn something new about the character or characters in the scene.

Don't be afraid to delete a scene when you're in the rewriting and editing phase. Maybe your plot has evolved, and the scene is no longer needed or no longer serves a purpose.

Two main formats for scenes

First format: Goal, Conflict, and Disaster: In this format, the main character wants something—achieving that is his goal. Conflicts always get in the way of him achieving that goal, and then, the scene ends with a disaster (or at least something going wrong) where the character doesn't reach his goal. When you have a scene ending with a disaster, it makes it easier to proceed to the reaction scene. You need disasters to keep the readers turning the pages.

Second format: Reaction, Dilemma, and Decision: After your character experiences a disaster, they will react. How do they feel? What are they thinking? They're in a dilemma after experiencing the disaster (or failure). What do they do now? They have options, but none of them are ideal. There are problems and risks with all the options they have to choose from. They are all difficult options. But they have to make a decision and do something. Doing nothing is the worst option of all.

After the characters make a decision, they move on to another goal, conflict, and disaster scene where they're trying to achieve a new goal (or maybe they're trying to achieve a previous goal in a different way).

Repeat these simple steps, and you'll soon have a finished book that flows smoothly and keeps your readers engaged and turning pages.

Two types of scenes: active and narrative

Your scenes will be a mixture of active drama and narrative summary scenes. A scene will be an active moment, and a summary will condense the situation and look at it from a distance. Your novel will need to have a mixture of these types of scenes to keep the reader involved.

The parts of a scene:

The following parts are not necessarily included in all scenes, but you need to think about each of these when writing a scene because each thing is happening whether you describe them in your scene or not.

Dialogue: Characters are speaking. What are they saying? The dialogue is the most critical part of many scenes and controls the whole scene.

Action: What is happening, what is moving, what is taking place?

Narrative: What do the characters think and feel about the situation? Including some narration in a book is why it's better than a movie most of the time. In a movie, it's not usually possible to describe or reveal what a character is feeling or thinking, but in your book, you can. In a movie, you would have to try to work this information into the dialogue, and most of the time, it would be awkward, but in a book, you can say, "He was feeling scared." You could also say, "he was thinking, 'Now is a good time to ask her to go to dinner with me.'"

Description: How do things look, sound, feel, smell, etc.? You may not always describe what a character is hearing or smelling in a scene, but explain what he is experiencing that is important or will become important later.

Backstory: What has happened previously to get to this point? Sometimes, a lot has happened, and sometimes, nothing or not much.

Your scenes will have different ratios of the above elements. Some scenes will consist of almost all dialogue, some mostly narrative, etc. There's no rule to define a scene. Go with what the story or situation calls for in each scene.

Beats, scenes, and chapters

A chapter may have only one scene or several. Most chapters are divided into two or three scenes. A beat is something that happens, but it's not long enough to expand into a scene. For example, someone dropped their phone. That's a beat but not a scene. Just like a chapter can have more than one scene, a scene can have more than one beat—and usually does.

In summary, one or more beats make up a scene, and one or more scenes make a chapter.

When rewriting and editing, you can (and usually will) delete beats, scenes, and sometimes chapters.

What marks the end of a scene? If you change the location or point of view, that would mark the end of a scene.

It used to be common to signal the end of a scene (or a scene break, as it's called) with a blank line, but now it's more common to insert a blank line and then include three astricts in a row with no spaces between them in that line. Here is an example of how you would mark a scene break:

***

If you're outlining your novel, giving each scene a descriptive name or title might be helpful. Some authors write scenes and then decide later how to arrange them and which chapter to place them in. Most scenes are stand-alone and can be moved around.

Writing scenes instead of chapters makes it easier to be productive when the words are not flowing freely. If you're struggling with a scene, you can jump over and write a scene you're more excited about. You can decide later where the scene will best fit.

Some writers work linearly, writing their novels straight through from beginning to end. Others find that writing scenes and then rearranging them and piecing them together later works better for them.

You might find that writing in a linear fashion for most of your book works best for you, but jumping off on a tangent sometimes and writing an unrelated scene when the mood strikes will keep you from getting stuck, and will allow you to be more productive.

The main takeaway from this chapter: When you write your story in scenes following the steps outlined in this chapter, you'll never have writer's block, and you'll end up with a story that flows logically, is easy to follow, and best of all, it will keep your readers intrigued and turning pages. Keep in mind that you can delete or move scenes around.

Chapter 11

How to Write Compelling Dialogue

"If I waited for perfection, I would never write a word."

~ Margaret Atwood

A good novel has to have compelling dialogue.

Dialogue is when two or more people talk with a clear purpose or agenda. People are always "shooting the breeze" with no agenda in the real world, but that should never happen in a novel.

Real-world speech meanders all over the place, but the dialogue in your novel should never wander aimlessly. It should always be a character with a purpose and an agenda talking to another character with a different agenda.

It's crucial that you know each person's purpose or agenda before you start writing the dialogue.

Writing dialogue can be fun

Writing dialogue is the most fun part of writing your novel. You get to use your imagination and creativity to bring your story to life.

Great dialogue can turn an ordinary novel into a captivating and enticing one. Improving your dialogue is the fastest, easiest, and best way to enhance any novel.

Dialogue can consist of only one word, and that one word can be more powerful than a long, rambling sentence. For example, if one person asks, "Does your wife know about this?" And the other responds, "Maybe." That one word says more than any long sentence could ever convey. That one word captures the reader's attention and makes them want to know more.

With dialogue, you can reveal what a character is thinking. For example, a comment can be followed by "she thought" instead of "she said." Dialogue can also reveal the speaker's mood: Are they sad, happy, angry, or frustrated?

Dialogue can provide information or describe feelings. It can reveal so much and make your story way more interesting than when you try to use narration to tell the reader everything.

You can use indirect dialogue in your book, such as, "I found out yesterday why he didn't tell me the whole truth."

Make your dialogue intriguing

Great dialogue can give the reader the sense they're eavesdropping. It's essential that your dialogue never sounds artificial.

An excellent way to learn how to write good dialogue is to listen to conversations in a coffee shop, in the break room at work, or anywhere else you can listen to people talking. What people say is not important—listen to the way they talk.

Another technique is to use your cell phone to record conversations. Then, listen to the conversations and pay attention to how often they cut each other off, use "uh," or change the subject. Make a note of these things and work them into your dialogue, and it will sound natural—but don'tover do it.

If your dialogue doesn't sound natural, it can destroy your story. When you write your dialogue well, it will grab the reader and pull them into the story. You must have compelling, correctly punctuated dialogue to have an intriguing story.

Dialogue can also help your readers get to know the characters better and learn about their lives.

How to write dialogue tags

Dialogue tags tell readers who is talking, but don't overuse them. Doing so will distract the reader from what's being said.

One of the best ways to use dialogue tags is to use the ones they don't notice. Most of the time, you should use "she said" and "he asked." Readers see these words so often their conscious minds won't realize they saw them.

Don't try to get creative with tags. If you need to describe volume, you can sometimes use words such as "whispered," "shouted," or "yelled," but use these sparingly.

You can place the tag before, after, or in the middle of your dialogue. Mix it up some.

It's important to punctuate your dialogue correctly

Don't worry about following grammar rules when you write dialogue because you're writing what your characters say. And people don't always use proper grammar when they speak. However, it is important to follow a few dialogue punctuation rules.

Writing and punctuating dialogue is the hardest part of writing a novel. Dialogue is where your book comes to life, but it can be a disaster if you don't punctuate your dialogue correctly.

Seven basic rules for punctuating dialogue

#1. Always enclose dialogue in double quotation marks.

#2. The closing punctuation mark always goes to the left of the quotation mark. That means a question mark or period always goes inside the closing quotation mark.

#3. When you change speakers, you always start a new paragraph.

#4. If your character is talking for more than one paragraph, you use opening quotes at the beginning of each paragraph but don't use closing quotes until after the end of the last paragraph.

#5. If you're writing dialogue and the sentence continues after a tag, don't start the rest of the sentence with an upper-case letter.

#6. Make sure you always use curly quotes and not straight quotes. Curly quotes will curve left or right, showing whether they're opening or closing quotation marks.

#7. Don't use a tag for every piece of dialogue. Dialogue tags are phrases and words such as *she said.* You want to use tags just often enough so the reader always knows who's talking.

Miscellaneous tips for writing dialogue

- Don't use long-winded dialogue.

- Keep your dialogue tight. After you write a dialogue section, go back and delete as many words and sentences as possible.

- Introduce a few memorable lines—especially for your main character, if possible. The easy way to do this is to have them say something profound and unexpected.

- Don't use dialogue as an information dump by trying to tell your readers a lot of information all at once. You can include some revealing information to intrigue your readers and keep them turning the pages, but don't provide too much information all at once. You can tell them more as the story moves along.

- Dialogue can be used to reveal previous events. For example, as they walked into the restaurant, Amy said, "Let's not mention anything about what happened last night." That statement sets the stage for more information to be revealed later about what happened last night. Comments like this will keep your readers turning pages.

- The best way to test your dialogue is to get a friend to role-play with you. Each of you can become a character. Read the dialogue back and forth and see how it sounds. Does it sound artificial? If someone overheard the two of you reading the dialogue, would they think you were having a conversation, or would they think you were reading a script?

The main takeaway from this chapter: Powerful dialogue is the key to a great novel. Spend a lot of time and effort crafting the best dialogue you can. Great dialogue will keep readers reading until the end, and it's the one thing that will have people recommending your book to their friends.

Chapter 12

Story Starters That Will Get You Going

"I'm writing a first draft and reminding myself that I'm simply shoveling sand into a box so later I can build castles."

~ Shannon Hale

Getting started is the hardest part of writing your novel. The easy way to get started is to start writing and rambling. Don't worry about what you're writing. Later, you will almost certainly delete the first few paragraphs you write.

Don't stress yourself out trying to write a perfect or profound opening or beginning. If you end up with a grand opening, it will be because it came to you later while writing your novel. It will never come to you in the beginning, so stop worrying about it.

I've included some "story starter" openings for different types of novels in this chapter. Use one of these to get your story started, and then keep rambling and writing. After you've written several pages, your story will begin to develop, and you'll be on your way to writing a great novel you'll be proud of.

If you follow this procedure, you'll find that it works much better than spending hours trying to come up with a profound opening sentence.

In this chapter, I've provided you with several opening lines you could use to start your story. Use one of these, or a variation of one of them, to start your story, and you'll be on your way. You can also use some of them for the beginning of a chapter.

It's time to start writing

Benjamin Franklin said, "Either write something worth reading or do something worth writing."

If you don't think you have done anything worth writing about, don't worry. The book you're writing is not about you anyway. It's about your main character, and he or she has done a lot of things worth writing about. They may have even done things they don't want you to discuss, but you might reveal some of them anyway as the story progresses.

Five steps to help you use these story starters

1. Scroll down to the genre for the kind of story you'll be writing.

2. Look at the list of story starter examples for that genre and find one that intrigues you.

3. Then, use one of the story starters you've found (or a modified version) as your first line, and you're on your way—you've started writing your novel.

4. Decide what happens next and what happens after that. The most important thing is to keep writing. Don't worry about whether what you're writing is good or bad. Most likely, it's terrible, but you can fix that later. Your job now is to write.

5. Remember that the first draft is you telling yourself the story. After you finish telling yourself the story, you can tweak it, put things in the proper order, tell it better, and edit it. Nora Roberts said, "You can fix anything except a blank page."

The important thing is to let the words flow. Don't think about doing any rewriting or editing. Keep writing. That's always easier said than done, but don't give up.

In the following section, I've given you some sample opening sentences for several types of novels. You can use them as they are or modify them to suit your story better.

Story starters for different genres

Romance

- I saw her the first day she came to work.

- I'm determined to find my one true love this summer.

- I saw her in the cafeteria and wondered who this new girl was. I had to meet her, and that was my first mistake.

- The prom was in two weeks, and I didn't have a date. Maybe I didn't have a date because I hadn't had the nerve to ask anyone.

- I never imagined what was in store for me when I decided to stop being so shy.

- Everyone told me he would cause me trouble, but no one told me how much.

- She was the most beautiful woman I had ever seen. Where did she come from? Did she have a boyfriend? Was she married?

Science fiction

- The two aliens were standing there looking at me. I had no idea what they were thinking. Maybe they knew what I was thinking.

- When I saw a genetically modified man for the first time, I couldn't believe my eyes.

- I began working on this in my basement, and strange things started happening.

- When I got the chance to volunteer to travel to a nearby galaxy, I jumped at the opportunity, but I never expected this would happen.

- The weird creature handed me a small blue rock and told me to always hold on to it. That's when my life started to change.

Mystery and crime

- Most people thought it was an accident, but I saw what happened.

- I was telling the truth, but I wasn't telling the whole truth.

- I didn't know who to tell but knew I had to tell someone immediately.

- I found the gun in the attic. That's when I knew everyone had it all wrong.

- Tammy had been missing for five days, and most people thought I had something to do with her disappearance.

- I was telling the truth, but the detectives didn't believe a word I said.

Humor

Good humor is hard for even experienced authors to write. It's okay to include some humor in your book, but remember that trying to make your whole book funny won't be easy.

- Everything was going fine until the rabbit got loose.

- I was excited to land a summer job but didn't know I would have to wear that.

- I thought it would be a fun prank, but things went haywire.

- I was sitting alone on the subway. How could anything go wrong?

- She didn't tell me the whole story. I've found that girls usually don't.

Westerns

Writing a Western novel could be easy. The plots are usually easy to follow. It's an excellent genre to choose if you enjoy it. You can watch Western movies on YouTube or Netflix or read Western novels and get several ideas.

Below are some story starter lines to help you start writing your Western.

- I was told that the West was not a safe place for a woman, but I didn't care. I was going anyway.

- The wagon train would pull out in two weeks, and I couldn't wait.

- Like everyone else, I wanted to find gold, but I knew it would be dangerous, and there was no guarantee of a strike.

- Pa said we might go to town on Saturday. I was beyond excited.

- Everything has changed since the railroad came to town—and most of the changes were not good.

- I considered returning to the East, but now Texas is my home. Raising cattle is all I know how to do.

Historical fiction

When writing historical fiction, you'll have to spend a lot of effort to keep the characters, setting, language, and many other things working together. And make sure everything you write is accurate. You'll probably need to do some research and read several books set in the period. Writing a historical novel can be a fun adventure if your heart's in it, but don't tackle this project lightly.

Here are some openings and story starter lines to get you going:

- Traveling to France was not at all what I expected.

- I arrived in America scared and excited at the same time.

- The ships would start arriving any day, and there were a lot of them.

- I had everything I owned in one bag when I boarded the steamship. My life was never going to be the same.

- If I was ever going to leave this town, now was the time to do it.

- I had a new job as a telegraph operator, and my life in this little town would be exciting.

Children's books

Writing children's books is different from writing your typical novel. I have friends who do it, and they love it. If you want to write children's books, there's much to learn. In addition to writing the story, you'll need several illustrations. If you need help with the illustrations, you can hire designers from Fiverr.com to do your graphics at a reasonable cost.

Start your story with a bang

Don't try to ease into your story. You should hit the ground running, if possible, with things happening almost immediately—maybe in the first sentence.

You need to have a conflict or tension point at the beginning of your story. It doesn't have to be big, and it doesn't have to be the central conflict of the book. Starting with the main character wanting something (or wanting something to happen) will help show how they think and act. It will also help readers get to know the main character and pull them into the story.

You don't want to start your story with pages and pages describing the setting with nothing happening. Your readers must connect with your main character in the opening pages.

The first chapter of your book must build some suspense. Every book needs some suspense to keep the readers involved. You want to give them something to be concerned about and look forward to, making them want to continue reading the book.

A final point: Flashbacks are hard to write. Even experienced writers find flashbacks challenging. They can also be confusing for readers unless they're handled carefully. My advice is to tell your story linearly without using flashbacks.

The main takeaway from this chapter: All writers have trouble starting their stories. They have trouble mainly because they're trying to write the perfect beginning. Realize that you will almost certainly delete, or at least totally change, the beginning you write. You may change it several times. So don't get stressed out about what you're writing for the beginning. Get busy writing. Writing is hard. Deleting text is easy.

Chapter 13

How to Hook Your Readers Early

"Make crime pay. Become a lawyer."

~ Will Rogers

The beginning of any good story should start with a hook. You haven't created a hook until you've piqued the reader's interest and got them to ask the question, "What's going to happen now?" Or have them ask, "Who or why?" Who shot the man, or who broke her heart, or why is he leaving?

Open with conflict

It doesn't have to be your main character learning that someone is planning to shoot the Pope or him finding Jimmy Hoffa's body and not knowing if he should tell anyone, but it does require that your main character is at odds with himself, someone, or something. Conflict keeps readers turning the pages. An opening comment that immediately reveals the hero's dilemma is also an excellent way to hook the reader.

Opening lines don't have to be memorable. Not many are. Do you remember the opening line of the last book you read? The ending needs to be memorable, but not the beginning. The purpose of opening lines is to hook the reader and pull them into the story. That's all.

Beginnings ask a question, and the ending answers it. What happens in the middle is your story.

Your hook is your first chance to impress the reader, and if you don't do an excellent job, it may be your last because they won't keep reading.

If you don't hook the reader and pull them into your story, it doesn't matter how great and memorable your ending is because they'll never see it.

Open with movement

Opening with movement will help to hook your reader. Instead of opening with the main character sitting and thinking, have him doing something, even if it's just getting into the car or walking down the sidewalk.

You don't have to hook your readers with the first sentence, but it's nice if you can hook them in the first two or three paragraphs. And, by all means, you need to hook them by the end of the first chapter.

As I said in Chapter 8, the setting you choose will help hook your readers, but you need more.

Every story needs a riveting hook to grab the readers and pull them into the story.

Don't spend a lot of time when you start writing trying to come up with a profound opening line or paragraph. When you come back to do the rewriting and editing, that's when you should spend time crafting your hook.

Your readers may not even finish the first chapter if your opening paragraph (or at least the first chapter) doesn't grab them with a gripping hook.

Writing your novel's first few pages is your book's most intimidating part. Writing the first sentence of your book doesn't have to be the first thing you write if it's giving you trouble. You could spend hours or days struggling with the opening sentence or first paragraphs.

During that time, you could have written two or three chapters. Start writing the section you're most excited about or the part that intrigues you most. Come back later and write your opening hook. Let your subconscious mind work on it, and a grand opening will come to you.

You need a memorable ending, and I'll discuss that topic in great detail in Chapter 18, but you don't need a memorable beginning. You need a powerful and compelling hook to pull your reader into the story. It doesn't need to be memorable, but it does have to be super enticing. That's what I will teach you in the rest of this chapter—how to write a riveting hook.

Conflict keeps your readers hooked

The plot or external conflict is about what happens, but the internal conflict is about why it matters. Keep these two points in mind as you write your story. They're important.

Internal conflict is simply desire being blocked by fear. Ask yourself what your main character desperately wants and how his fear keeps him from pursuing it.

The beginning of your novel needs to have conflict or tension. It doesn't have to be the central conflict of the story. But it needs to intrigue the readers and pull them into the story. It will also give the readers an idea about how the characters think, their motivation, and how they react to situations.

Character development in the opening paragraphs is more important than describing the setting. A good hook requires the readers to care about the character before they care about what happens to him.

Your hook should focus on who the story is about and why "what's happening" matters to them. Why it matters is more important than what's happening.

For example, if your main character breaks his ankle, that's bad, but it's a lot worse if he's the star high school basketball player and it's a week before the tournament is scheduled to start. It matters even more if how he played in the tournament would significantly influence whether he gets a college scholarship or not.

As you can see, why it matters is way more important to your story than what happened.

Always show why what is happening to your main character is so important to him.

When you read a book, watch a movie or TV show, and find yourself quickly pulled into the story (or hooked, as writers call it), stop and see if you can determine exactly what they did to get you hooked. Note the technique they used, and you can use a similar method in one of your stories. We can all learn from other writers.

Take the time to develop your characters *before* your plot kicks in. Readers won't care much about what happens to the character until they know him.

You must quickly show the reader *why* what happened to the protagonist or main character matters. Avoid describing the world the character is in before it matters to him.

Anything that successfully gets your reader to keep reading your book will be a good hook. Rather than trying to find out what works by trial and error, I will give you some guidelines and proven techniques to help you get your hook right the first time.

Effective ways to create a hook

- Tell something interesting about your character's circumstance—an unusual occupation, a disability, having magical powers, or being unusually young or old.

- Raise a question the readers want an answer to, such as: Why did Bill come home so late last night? Why did Sarah steal the car? Why does he want to buy a gun? Why did Rick decide to drop out of school?

Who shot the maid? What did she know? Some of these questions will be answered early in the book, and some may not be answered until near the end.

- Put your character in a life-changing situation.

- Have one character interrogate another character to get information he doesn't want to give.

- Make the reader want to know more about your character.

- You could start with a cliffhanger with the main character literally hanging over a cliff.

- You could have a couple who have each already hired a hitman to kill the other. Did they hire the same hitman?

- Quickly introduce meaningful internal conflict within the character. What is he struggling with?

- Who is Barbara visiting in prison every week, and why?

- Start with the instant the character's ordinary world is interrupted. For example, start your story where the main character gets shot—the things he did before that doesn't matter. Later, you can fill in why he got shot or the reasons why he might have gotten shot and who might have shot him.

- You need to create suspense and urgency in the first few pages of your book. That's part of your hook.

Your first chapter should be reasonably short and end with a cliffhanger. It doesn't have to be an earth-shattering cliffhanger—a minor one-sentence one will do.

The main takeaway from this chapter: Go against conventional wisdom, and don't spend a lot of time trying to write the perfect hook for your book. Review the information in this chapter occasionally as you write your book, and your hook will come to you later. As you write your story, it will become apparent to you what your hook should be.

Chapter 14

How to Structure Your Story

"Suppose you were an idiot, and suppose you were a member of Congress, but I repeat myself."

~ Mark Twain

Having the right story and scene structure will allow you to perfectly time your story's major events. In real life, time is nature's way of keeping everything from happening at once, but in your book, the structure of your story is your way of making things happen when you want them to—not too fast or slow.

The first part of your story structure is the hook, but in the previous chapter, we discussed how important it was to have a strong hook and how to create one, so now we can move on.

Where should your story start?

Of course, your book should start with a hook, but you must immediately start the story after the hook. We discussed story starter phrases in Chapter 12, and here's some more important information about how to start your story.

Stories are about people. If you don't have people, you don't have a story. So you must introduce your main character at the beginning—maybe even in the first sentence or first paragraph. If you can make it part of the hook, that would be even better.

An old cliche in the theater also applies to writing scenes in a novel: **"Come in late and leave early."** It means don't spend too much time providing background information that's not needed yet. Start with the action. Then, end the scene as soon as possible. Don't ramble on.

As your story progresses, you'll need to reveal more about your characters, their desires, their dilemmas, and the setting. Of course you'll also need to weave in some intriguing subplots. Next, you'll move on to the climax, resolution, and ending. This is an oversimplified description of the structure of your story. It's crucial that all these parts are carefully included.

You can start your story with, "Amy walked into the room and shot the delivery man, making a clean hole in his bright yellow envelope." or "Bill threw his wedding ring at Jamie as he walked out the door." The reader doesn't need to immediately know all the backstories of how the characters got to this point. That can come later.

Some writers use chapters strictly for pacing rather than structure, sometimes putting the break inside a scene to keep you turning pages.

How do chapters fit into the structure of your story?

Chapters can be long or short, and some books don't even use chapters. I like short chapters—both as a reader and a writer. Writers use many criteria to determine how and when to start a new chapter.

One popular and often-used technique is to start a new chapter whenever the main character makes an important decision or choice. If your main character moves around a lot, you could start a new chapter whenever he moves to a new location.

How do you structure a chapter?

It depends on where you are in your story and what you want the chapter to accomplish.

The start of a chapter should always pull the reader in, but it should also flow naturally from the previous chapter. There are several ways to do this.

If there are things you need to explain from the end of the previous chapter, you could start with a short narrative. If the last chapter ended with a cliffhanger, you could pick the new chapter up in the middle of a scene and return to the action. If you want to start a new scene, you could begin with some dialogue to get the scene going with some action.

Regardless of how you start a new chapter, it should be engaging and quickly pull the reader back into the story.

The story should start to change distinctively by the middle of the chapter. If there is no change by the end of the chapter, you need to modify the chapter or decide it's unnecessary and delete it. The goal of every chapter is to change the story.

You don't want problems resolved in the middle of a chapter. You want the tension to escalate throughout the chapter so the reader will keep reading.

If you have trouble structuring your chapter, treat it like a short story. Every chapter can be considered a short story. It should have a critical development that moves the main story along.

You don't want your character to experience success or failure at the end of every chapter. Just like in life, we experience high points and low points. Your character should, too. The end of a chapter is an excellent place to resolve some of the tension, but you don't want to fix all of it until the end of the book.

When you see a change from the beginning to the end of a chapter, that's a good sign that you have structured the chapter properly and are ready to move on to the next chapter.

Structuring your story will not inhibit your creativity

Your first thought might be that structure will hinder your ability to be creative. If you write a detailed outline, I can see how you might think that would somewhat put a damper on your creativity. But don't worry—it won't happen.

Mark Twain probably knew a few things Huck Finn might do while floating down the Mississippi River on a raft. Or maybe he didn't even know what was around the next bend in the river or who Huck Finn would run into. And I doubt if he had any idea what would happen to him.

If you structure your story correctly, there won't be the saggy middle that is the death of so many novels. If your story dies in the middle, your readers will stop reading and never get to the profound and amazing ending you worked so hard to perfect.

Flashback and flashforward scenes

Be careful with flashback and flashforward scenes. These are hard to write, and if you don't do a good job, you can confuse the reader, and they will put the book down. Ask yourself if a flashback or flashforward scene is necessary. Can you structure your story differently so these scenes are not required?

A flashback and a backstory are not the same thing. The backstory is narration that will tell the reader how the character got to where he is, why he feels the way he does, and maybe why he will take the action he's about to take.

The backstory can be crucial to your story, but keep it short. Don't ramble and drag it out.

A flashback lets the reader figure these things out for themselves, but in most cases, it's better to tell the reader the backstory.

Your story must have a climax. Build up to it, and make it fast and big when you get to it. You don't want a so-so climax. When you build up to the climax, drop it like a bomb. Don't ease into it.

The main takeaway from this chapter: Your story must be structured and organized. You don't want your story to bounce around in every direction. Structuring your story or working from an outline does not inhibit your creativity.

Chapter 15

Write Engaging Descriptions

"Description begins in the writer's imagination but should finish in the reader's."

~ Stephen King

Write descriptions well, and you can make characters and settings come to life.

Writing vivid and engaging descriptions can be challenging. It's difficult to know what to include and what to leave out. You don't want to do an information dump and load your readers with information and facts they don't need to know yet.

Feed them information gradually as they need to know it, and try to do it by working the information into the dialogue and the story. When the description is part of the story, the readers will not even realize you're describing things to them.

Your writing style doesn't matter

When you describe people, settings, and things, you may wonder if you're doing it in the right tone. What is your writing style? What should it be? The answer is simple: It doesn't matter.

It doesn't matter because you're not describing anything. Your character is. How would he describe things? When you tell your story from the main character's point of view, it's their voice describing things. The more you can become your character, the easier it will be for you to tell their story.

Try to hear their voice in your head when you're writing. Do they have an accent? Can you hear their accent in your head? Be careful using accents in your writing. It could backfire if you're not good at it. It always amazes me when Hollywood writers try to create a character from the Deep South. It's obvious they have never been in the South or heard someone with an authentic Southern accent talk. Their efforts sound artificial.

Work your descriptions into the dialogue

When you can do that, the readers won't realize you're describing things. Mixing your description in with the dialogue will keep the story moving. The reader may see the setting in his mind and not even realize you've described it to him.

It's essential to make sure your reader can picture where the action is taking place. Make them feel like they're in the scene. A good description is always clear. It's not just what a place looks like. How does it smell, sound, and feel?

When describing things, keep it simple. You don't need to explain everything. Describe only what is essential to the story or will become important later. When possible, make your description an integral part of your story.

A clear description of your characters and settings will help bring the characters to life and make the settings seem real.

Make your descriptions exciting and more original

Use words that describe things the reader can see. Don't use abstract words that your readers can't picture. Words such as loss, happiness, sadness, grief, and peace are not descriptive.

Use strong nouns and verbs. Instead of saying he put on his shoes, say he put on his black alligator cowboy boots. When you describe something, you want the readers to picture it in their minds.

Give specific details. Don't be vague. Instead of saying he was changing the tire on his car, you could say he was changing the tire on his Fathom Green 1969 Corvette or his new electric Tesla Model 3. Readers can picture these cars. This description also tells the readers more about the character, what he likes, and what interests him.

When you describe your character taking a walk in the evening, does she enjoy the moon and the twinkling stars or complain about the mosquitos and the hot, muggy air? Each description tells the readers something about the setting and the character.

Add comments in your descriptions about things moving. This will make the setting come to life. For example, you could describe a bird flying across the sky, leaves on the trees blowing in the breeze, or a cat jumping upon the sofa.

Use powerful descriptive words

You don't want to use words your readers don't know the meaning of. But when you use words they know but don't often use, it will work wonders in your descriptions.

Here are 11 underused descriptive words:

- Thud—as in a loud noise

- Rumbling

- Filthy

- Savory

- Toxic

- Hazy

- Uncanny

- Musty

- Dilapidated

- Cuddly

Can you see how these words would cause the reader to see a picture or experience a feeling, smell, or taste?

Where and when is the story taking place?

If it's important to your story, readers will want to know where and when your story is taking place.

If your story is set in the current time, that will be obvious, but if it takes place in 1865, just after the end of the Civil War, when the Wright Brothers were building and testing their first plane, or in the future in the year 2,300, you need to make this clear.

If you choose the right words, you can tell your readers a lot in one sentence. You want them to picture the scene and what you're describing, but don't drag out your description.

How to describe emotions

People try to hide most of their emotions in public, so to make your character seem real, don't overdo their expressions of emotion. You can describe some emotions when the situation calls for it.

When you describe your character's emotions or reactions to a situation, think about how they would act. You want your character to come across as a real person. They can have quirks and their own personality but don't make them act over dramatic if that's not their nature.

Three final points about writing descriptions

#1. Write compelling descriptions of your characters. You want your descriptions to help your readers feel like they know the characters. Your description should be more than just a physical description. It should also include their goals and ambitions, what they're afraid of or worried about, and what they're thinking and feeling.

#2. Provide vivid descriptions of settings. Your readers need to be able to picture where the story takes place. Is it on a beach, in the living room, at a university, or downtown in a large city?

#3. If you're describing a fictional place, visit a similar real place if possible. Pretend it's the place where your story takes place and describe it. Don't rely totally on your imagination if you don't have to.

The main takeaway from this chapter: Learning how to write engaging descriptions will immediately improve your writing. The key is to describe settings, characters, and scenes without the readers knowing you're doing it. Working your descriptions into the dialogue and the story is the best way to describe things. You don't want to do an information dump in a long section of narration. You'll bore your readers when you do this.

Chapter 16
Conflicts are the Key

"The glow of one warm thought is worth more than money."

~Thomas Jefferson

Without conflict, there is no story—at least, not one anyone would want to read.

Your main character wants something, but he runs into some obstacles. That's conflict, and that's your story. In all conflicts, there are stakes or things to lose.

The stakes may be so high that they're life-threatening, or they may be risking a speeding ticket if they drive this fast all the way home. The higher the stakes, the greater the conflict.

If your character always succeeds, your story won't be enjoyable. You need your character to experience some failures and setbacks. You want them to fail more than they succeed.

You've heard the old saying, "There's nothing to write home about." If that describes your story, you don't have a story.

Whether you're writing a book about romance, crime, science fiction, a western, or something else, your story must build to a climax where the main character finds himself in a more or less impossible situation. This is the kind of conflict you want in your story.

You need a dude with a problem

Start your story with a main character who has a problem. He wants something, but obstacles are in his way. Let the story build to a climax where the situation looks impossible, and then there needs to be a believable but unexpected resolution.

Your main character must experience several conflicts, setbacks, and dilemmas on his journey to reach his goal. He will have to make decisions, and some of his choices will probably do more harm than good and take him farther from achieving his goal. How your main character deals with all of his conflicts, setbacks, decisions, and dilemmas is your story.

If you feel your story is falling flat and dull, it's most likely because of a lack of conflict. Readers love conflict. Adding conflict to a story is like adding seasoning to food. It gives it flavor and adds excitement.

You never want your story to be boring. You want to keep your readers excited and eager to know what will happen next. If they get bored, they'll put your book down and not pick it up again. You never want to bore your readers.

You want your readers to be so involved in your story that they forget to feed the cat.

All stories must have conflicts

Never forget that without conflict, there's no story. We try to avoid conflicts in the real world, but readers can't seem to get enough of them in the books they read.

Your story will need both internal and external conflicts. There's a difference.

Internal and external conflicts

External conflict is what happens, and internal conflict is why it matters.

External conflict occurs when something happens to the main character, such as when he loses his job, misses his flight, or runs out of ammunition.

Internal conflict occurs when a person is facing a moral or spiritual dilemma or decision. For example, he can close the sale if he tells a small lie.

Your main character must have flaws if he's going to come across as authentic. Nobody is perfect. Maybe he has a temper, walks with a limp, or is colorblind. These faults could play into your story at some point.

Show—don't tell

What does this mean? It's something important that new writers screw up all the time. If you tell the readers everything, there's nothing to pull them into the story. It's better to describe the situation (through dialogue, if possible) and let the readers figure out the point you're trying to make.

You want to give your readers an active role in experiencing your story. The easy way to do this is to find ways to show them as many things as possible rather than telling them.

Here are examples:

- Don't say she was pretty. Say, "Every guy in the room turned to look at her when she walked across the room with her long blonde hair swaying."

- Instead of telling them that Sarah was angry, say, "She grabbed her purse and slammed the door as she bolted out of the room." Does this leave any doubt about whether she was angry or not?

- Instead of saying he was clumsy, say, "He would trip over his own shadow."

Dialogue is another excellent way to show rather than tell the reader something. When you work information into the dialogue, the story can move along while you still get your point across. You can let the reader deduce many things rather than spoon-feeding them every little detail. Your readers are more intelligent than you think.

You can use narration to tell the reader some things, but keep it brief and let the story move on. You don't want to call attention to your writing. Ideally, you want the reader to forget he's reading. When you can do this, you have written a great story.

After all the conflict and dilemmas, there has to be a climax where everything looks hopeless, and then you reveal the unexpected resolution. You must include all of these things to have a good story.

The main takeaway from this chapter: Conflict is what makes your story. Without conflict, there's not much of a story. In real life, we try hard to avoid conflict, but when we read a novel, we crave it. Conflict keeps readers involved in a story and keeps them turning the pages. Your story must build to a climax and end with a realistic but unexpected resolution, with everything resolved.

Chapter 17
Suspense and Climax

"Sometimes I write better than I can."

~ Ernest Hemingway

Your story needs suspense to build to the point where everything looks impossible, and the reader wonders if your character will ever get out of this. This is the climax your story has been building to.

A story that doesn't have conflicts, problems, suspense, and a great climax wouldn't be much of a story. The climax you write is the make-or-break moment in your story. If you have a ho-hum climax, you'll have a ho-hum story.

If you want to keep your reader turning the pages, your novel must contain suspense.

Suspense can be described as the anticipation readers feel while waiting for something they think is about to happen. Your reader is concerned about your character, wondering if he will be okay.

Three things are necessary to create suspense

1. **You have to have a looming disaster.** It doesn't have to be life-threatening. For example, a looming

catastrophe in your character's world could be getting fired or running out of gas. Running out of gas would be an even bigger looming catastrophe if he was in an airplane.

2. **Make the readers wait for the event.** This causes anticipation and heightens the suspense. There's no suspense if you reveal the outcome almost immediately. You have to build up to the event.

3. **Suspense has to have a clear endpoint.** Good or bad, something has to happen, and the suspense has to end.

Suspense is usually a short event, but it can drag out over a few chapters or the whole book. Who committed the crime is an example of suspense that could last for most of the book. This is called long-term suspense.

Whether you have long-term suspense or not, you also need short-term suspenseful events. Short-term suspense is a brief time of heightened anxiety, usually lasting one chapter or less.

There is suspense anytime something is about to happen. It doesn't have to be something terrible. It could be something funny or romantic. For example, is he finally going to ask her to marry him?

How to build suspense

To build suspense, you need to have your reader invested in the outcome and craving an answer. You can help make this happen by leaving clues that the reader won't recognize as a clue at the time but will remember and recognize after the event occurs. Then they will think, *Why didn't I see that coming?*

You don't want the outcome to be predictable when you resolve a suspenseful situation. You want a believable but unexpected resolution.

The classic and easiest way to create suspense is to put a character the readers care about in danger. This technique can't be used in the early part of the book. It must be used after readers are invested in and care about the character. The more your readers care about a character, the easier it is to create suspenseful situations.

Long-term and short-term suspense

You need both long-term and short-term suspense and can have them simultaneously. In a murder mystery, for example, there could be long-term suspense where the main character is accused of murder, and it takes the whole book to resolve that he didn't do it. At the same time, several short-term suspenseful situations could take place.

It's also crucial that the character doesn't have an easy and obvious way out of the situation. The situation needs to look hopeless to be suspenseful, and you don't want the reader to see the resolution coming.

Sometimes, you want the suspense to be so intense that your reader will forget about other things they should be doing. To do that, you must create characters your reader cares about before they'll be concerned about what happens to them.

The more your reader feels like they know your characters, their thoughts, goals, fears, desires, concerns, and worries, the more they'll care about what happens to them.

Different types of suspense

Not all suspense has to involve something dangerous or life-threatening about to happen to your beloved character. Suspense can be about whether the football team captain will ask Jill to the prom when he sees her this afternoon.

After all, he did tell her when he hurried past her as she came out of history class that he wanted to ask her something after school.

Slowing things down can build suspense

You want to make your readers wait while the tension builds, so don't move things along too fast.

One way to slow things down and build suspense is to use short sentences. Mixing in a few one- or two-word sentences will do the trick.

The words you use to describe what's happening, the sounds, and what the characters are thinking can all help build suspense. To create extra suspense, you may want to use a few more adjectives than you usually use.

Mark Twain said, "When you catch an adjective, kill it."

Maybe he didn't mean to kill all adjectives because he didn't kill all of his adjectives. He used some, but he used them sparingly. When you don't use many adjectives, the ones you use are powerful. An adjective is frequently propping up a boring verb. Find a more powerful or descriptive verb, and it won't need the help.

You can also heighten suspense by dropping clues in earlier paragraphs.

You can say things like there has been an increase in crime lately, especially after dark. You can add that Ashley has recently heard strange sounds outside her house. And now that the power has gone off, she's getting scared.

You can throw in the clue that her cell phone battery has died in an earlier paragraph. It wasn't important when you mentioned the dead battery, but now it's becoming critical. Her cell phone battery is dead, and she doesn't have a way to charge it. Nothing has happened yet, but suspense and tension are building. Give enough clues to let your reader figure out that something's about to happen before your hero does.

Suspense keeps the reader turning pages

It's easy to let your story get uninteresting and boring in the middle. Don't let your story die in the second act. Adding subplots and suspense can keep you and the reader interested in the story. If you don't keep the readers excited and engaged in the middle, they'll never see your surprise ending.

If you become bored with your book, you can be sure your reader will be too. The worst thing a writer can do is bore their readers.

Many writers spend a lot of time and effort writing the openings and endings of their novels, but they get bored and discouraged when writing the middle. You can never have a good book without a good middle. Don't forget this.

Here is a general outline to keep the suspense in your story. If you follow this formula, you won't have trouble deciding what to write next to keep the story and the suspense going from the beginning to the end.

The basic flow of all great novels

- Start by describing what the main character wants or wants to happen.

- What obstacles are standing in his way?

- What actions is he taking to try to do something about overcoming the obstacles?

- Sometimes, everything he tries to do to fix the problem only makes things worse until everything appears hopeless. You need these failures to make him look human so the readers will feel his pain and bond with him.

- End your story with a unique ending the reader

didn't see coming. And, of course, your ending has to resolve all the problems that have been introduced.

That's the main plot (or outline) of your story.

The main takeaway from this chapter: All stories need some suspenseful events to keep the reader interested and wanting to know what will happen next. Using subplots is an excellent way to include suspense in your novel. Suspense is created anytime the reader waits for an answer or for something he thinks is going to happen. Regardless of the kind of story you're writing, make sure there is an adequate dose of suspense.

Chapter 18

How to End Your Book

"There is no real ending. It's just the place where you stop the story."

~ Frank Herbert

All writers struggle with how to end their books—and they should because how you end your story is one of the most critical parts of your story. You want a "surprising yet inevitable" ending. One, the reader didn't see it coming, but once it does, it's obvious it had to happen.

Your ending should be memorable and not predictable. You want an ending that will have them talking about your book and recommending it to their friends for weeks or months after they finish reading it. If your readers don't remember the ending, they won't remember your book.

You need an ending that will leave a lasting impression on your readers

It's easy to kill off the bad guy or have the couple finally fall in love, get married, and end your book, but that's a cop-out. You can do better than that. Your readers probably saw that coming halfway through the book.

You have to wrap up all the loose ends unless you plan to write a sequel, and I recommend you don't do that with your first book. If you leave anything unresolved, your readers will notice it. They will be disappointed, and you'll likely get some bad reviews. And for sure, they won't be recommending your book to their friends.

A powerful ending

You have to have a mighty climax and resolution to have an excellent ending to your novel. These are *not* the same thing.

The climax is the most intense time in your story. It's when the conflict comes to a head. It happens near the end of your book, but you need the climax to occur before the last chapter.

In the last chapter, you have the resolution. This is when everything gets resolved and wrapped up.

The last chapter is the most crucial chapter in your book. It's your readers' last impression of your book before they will, hopefully, post a review on Amazon. The last chapter can make or break your book. You want them to feel impressed and satisfied.

A few more comments about ending your story

Make sure everything is resolved, including the subplots. Don't wait until the last chapter to fix all the subplots. Some subplots can be resolved in earlier chapters. Don't ever introduce a new character in the late chapters.

For example, in a crime story, the killer can't turn out to be somebody who shows up near the end of the story. It has to be somebody who has been around since the beginning. You would like the reader to say, "I didn't see that coming," not, "How the heck was I supposed to know that?"

When everything is resolved, stop writing

Your resolution and ending need to be more than "They lived happily ever after," but don't drag it out over multiple chapters. Your last chapter should be short. Don't ramble on. Wrap things up. After everything is resolved, your story is over. Stop writing.

You hooked the reader and pulled them into your story with the conflict. Now, you have to make sure the ending fully resolves that conflict. Your readers are invested in your story and main character and are craving a satisfying ending.

How to tell if your book ending sucks

Ask yourself these four questions about the ending of your book. Unless you can answer "yes" to all of them, your ending sucks, and your readers will be disappointed and unhappy. Here are the questions:

#1. Does your novel have a satisfying resolution to the central conflict?

#2. Did you wrap up all loose ends?

#3. Did you have a logical but unpredictable ending?

#4. Does your last paragraph leave your readers with the feeling you want them to have?

How do your readers feel after reading your book?

What do your readers feel after reading the last sentence of your book? Ask your beta readers how the ending made them *feel*. This is important. Listen carefully to the feedback you get from your beta readers when you ask them this question.

Most people don't remember how a book begins, but they remember how it ends. You want your book to have a memorable ending that will leave a lasting impression on your readers so they'll talk about your book and recommend it to their friends.

A book without a clear climax and resolution will frustrate the reader. The readers will not feel the satisfaction they deserve or were expecting.

Closing thoughts on endings

Your ending must be worthy of the time and money the reader has invested. It has to be memorable and emotionally satisfying. You want the reader to be surprised by the ending but also want them to feel that they should have seen it coming. That will happen if you leave a few clues along the way. But don't leave too many clues—your readers may be more savvy than you think.

Orson Wells said, "If you want a happy ending, that depends, of course, on where you stop your story."

Your book doesn't have to have a happy ending, but it does need to have a memorable ending.

The main takeaway from this chapter: Many writers sweat over trying to write the perfect opening line or beginning to their novel, but can you tell me the opening line of the last book you've read lately? Probably not, because people don't often remember the beginning of a story. The opening lines of a novel are essential to hook the reader and pull them into the story, but after that, they're no longer critical. The ending is what needs to be memorable.

If a book has a memorable ending, readers will talk about it and recommend it to their friends for weeks or months after reading it. When your ending does this, you've nailed it. This will make your book successful.

Chapter 19

Final Thoughts on Writing Your Novel

"Imagination is everything. It is the preview of life's coming attractions."

~ Albert Einstein

Writing a novel is a process. In this chapter, I've outlined the major parts of the process.

Even before you start writing, you must come up with a story idea you're passionate about. If you're not excited about the story you're about to write, you can be sure you will never finish writing your novel. Even if you did somehow struggle and finish your book, no one would read much of it because if you're not excited about it, your readers won't be either.

Plunge your main character into serious trouble immediately

Ramp things up and show that everything he does to resolve the situation makes things worse. This continues until his predicament appears completely hopeless.

This process is essential. You don't want the reader to see an easy way for your hero to escape his situation. You don't want the reader to think, why doesn't he crawl out the window he left open, use the gun he hid in his boot, or use the spare key he keeps in his wallet?

Ramp up the tension until things look utterly hopeless

You want things to look so bad for your main character that even you wonder how you will write your way out of the situation. When you start to feel this way, you know you've done an excellent job of backing your hero into a corner with no escape. Your ability to make your lead character fall into a hopeless situation will make or break you as a novelist.

Don't be tempted to give your hero a break and provide a miracle. Don't write an easy way out by having the hero suddenly remember where he hid the spare key.

The more bleak and hopeless you can make the situation, the more powerful and memorable your ending will be.

Your novel is fiction, but your story must be believable

Do your research. Include some facts the reader didn't know. Make sure your facts are accurate. Research will add flavor to your writing.

Mark Twain said, "The only difference between reality and fiction is that fiction needs to be credible."

How you handle the POV is critical

Generally, you should limit your POV to one person per scene. One per chapter would be even better, and one for your whole novel would be the best if you're writing your first novel. The more times you change the POV, the harder your book will be to write, and the easier it will be for the reader to get confused.

Remember, you're writing your first novel, so don't make things complicated for yourself.

Start your novel with action

Something important should be happening. Don't start with a lot of scene setting and background information. When you first meet someone, do you want to know their background information or how they got into their situation? You're not interested until you get to know the person better. The same is true for your readers. They don't care about the main character yet.

The movie wasn't as good as the book. How many times have you heard this said or experienced it yourself? There are two big reasons for this.

1. The first reason is that books tell the story with dialogue and narration. Movies use almost all dialogue, so getting a point across can sometimes be awkward.

2. The second and biggest reason is that Hollywood can't compete with the reader's imagination when

describing a scene or character. In your novel, you want to give the reader some description, but not too much. And for sure, don't use an illustration. Provide a brief description, then leave it up to the reader's imagination to fill in the details.

Conflict drives fiction

Don't make things too easy for your hero. Consider doing the opposite. What if he is involved in an accident, his car and cell phone are stolen, he has lost his job, and he doesn't have the money to pay his rent? And to top it off, his dog has run away. The more trouble he's in, and the more conflict you can ramp up, the easier it is to pull the reader into your story.

Also, the more impossible the hero's situation, the more powerful and memorable your ending can be—if you do it right.

The main takeaway from this chapter: Several important parts must be included in a story to make it truly great. And that's what you want. You don't want to write a so-so book. You want to write a great novel you'll be proud to put your name on.

Chapter 20

Rewriting, Editing, and Proofreading

"When your story is ready for rewrite, cut it to the bone. Get rid of every ounce of excess fat. This is going to hurt."

~ Stephen King

You can never write a good book without freeing your inhibitions and letting the words flow.

If you don't think your first draft is crappy, it probably means you were way too critical while you were writing and didn't let the words flow. If you aren't embarrassed by it, you were trying to edit as you went along. When you do this, your book will sound awkward and stiff.

Turn your rough manuscript into a masterpiece

To do this, you'll need to do a lot of rewriting. After you've finished proofreading, rewriting, and editing your manuscript several times, it's time to turn it over to a professional proofreader if you can afford one.

A good editor would provide more help than a proofreader. An editor could help you find and correct plotholes and other problems with your story, but a good editor would cost you $2,000 to $3,000. A proofreader is much less expensive. They charge about $300 to $400, depending on the length of your book.

Using a good proofreader is money well spent, but I'm not sure about hiring an editor. I know any book could be improved by a good editor, but would the book be improved enough to earn you the extra $2,000 to $3,000 an editor would cost? Maybe so. It depends on how much help your book needs. I don't spend the money for an editor.

If your budget can't handle hiring a proofreader, you'll need to have even more friends to be beta readers. You don't pay beta readers.

Rewriting is hard but necessary

Writing a book is fun, but I wouldn't call the process of rewriting it fun. Rewriting is hard work. Rewriting will involve a lot of deleting, rearranging, and rewording sections. It's mentally draining.

You can't proofread or edit your own writing and shouldn't try. At least, that's the conventional wisdom. But as I've said before, conventional wisdom is wrong about many things.

Here's how to do your own proofreading and editing

Begin by letting your manuscript set for at least a week—two weeks would be even better. Start with the attitude that nothing is sacred. Delete all of the fluff and rambling. You'll probably need to cut out sentences, paragraphs, and sometimes even a whole chapter. This is called making your writing tight. If a section doesn't seem to fit in, maybe it's because it doesn't belong there.

There's a phrase writers use called "kill your darlings." It means sometimes you'll have sections you think you've written well, and you don't want to get rid of them, but if they're not helping your story or don't fit in, you have to delete them. In other words, "kill your darlings."

Accept that your manuscript won't be perfect when you finish editing it. And everything wouldn't be correct if you had hired a professional proofreader and editor. When rewriting and editing your manuscript, your job is not to make it perfect but to make it better. It's because the bits of your writing you're most fond of are the ones that need to go. Sometimes because you can't be objective about them, but often because they look like "writing" instead of your story.

Having good beta readers is a blessing

The more people you can get to be a beta reader and read your manuscript, the better. No one person, not even the professionals, will catch all the mistakes in your manuscript.

Friends who will stroke your ego and tell you how great your book is are not the people you want for your beta readers. You want people who will read your manuscript carefully and be ruthless in criticizing it and pointing out mistakes and parts they didn't understand, had trouble following, or found boring.

You will need at least three or four beta readers—more would be even better. Remember that some people who promise to read your manuscript will never get around to it.

They probably had good intentions, but life gets in the way, and things come up that are more important to them than reading your manuscript.

You don't have to make all the changes your beta readers suggest. Some of the recommendations will be to fix errors, but some will be more about how they think you can say something better. Consider all the suggestions your beta readers make, but it's your book and your decision about what gets changed and what doesn't.

Errors will be discovered after your book is published

Finding mistakes after your book is printed is not as big a problem as it used to be. You can make changes to your eBook and printed book in a matter of minutes at no cost. Then, when someone orders either version of your book the next day, they'll receive the latest corrected version.

Amazon does "print-on-demand," meaning they don't print a book until someone orders it, but it usually ships the same day.

My secret technique for finding errors in my book

The technique is simple—have your computer read your manuscript aloud. I've never failed to find mistakes when

I do this. I call this technique a secret because almost nobody uses it, but it works wonders.

It works because your mind knows what the words are trying to say. Your subconscious mind will insert missing words or change the wrong word to the correct word, and your brain will hear what your manuscript was trying to say. MS Word, LibreOffice, or another computer program can use a text-to-voice feature to read your manuscript to you as you follow along, looking at the printed text. It's important that you follow along, looking at the text as you hear the words read aloud to you.

You can search Google for free programs if you don't already have a text-to-voice program on your computer. You'll find plenty of them. Your phone most likely has one built in, and it may sound a lot more natural than the other options.

When should you stop editing?

Your book will never be perfect, but you can't keep tweaking it forever. That's fine when you're fixing mistakes, but you may find yourself making changes because you think the new version sounds better. You may be doing more harm than good. The more changes you make, the less the book will sound like you.

When you edit your manuscript, look for factual errors. Proofreaders and beta readers are not skilled at finding factual mistakes, and they're usually not even looking for them. They're also probably not experts on the topic of your book, so don't expect them to find all of the factual errors. That's your job.

Eventually, you'll have to decide that your manuscript is "good enough." Go ahead and publish it, and then correct the errors that will be found after publication.

The main takeaway from this chapter: Rewriting, editing, and proofreading will turn your rough manuscript into a polished masterpiece. I spend way more time rewriting and editing than writing the first draft. Let your manuscript marinate for a week or longer, and then spend a lot of time rewriting and editing. Do a good job of rewriting, and you'll have a great book you'll be proud to put your name on.

Chapter 21

Lost, Confused, or Overwhelmed? Start Here

"Words are our most inexhaustible source of magic."

~ J. K. Rowling

In this book, I've given you a lot of information about how to write your novel. It's too much information to comprehend all at once. I understand that. Writing a book is a major undertaking, but you can do it. You have the information in this book to guide you through every step in the process.

A writer friend once told me he sometimes thinks he should put his quill back in the goose where it would be more useful. I've felt the same way at times. It's easy to get overwhelmed, but let's take it one step at a time.

What should you do first?

There are so many ways to start writing your novel that it's easy to get completely overwhelmed. Maybe you feel like you're experiencing information overload.

Since you've read this far, you're obviously serious about writing your novel. You may not have the confidence yet, but you have the knowledge you need.

An overview of how to start writing your book

You may not need an outline. Many famous writers don't work from an outline. Of course, some do. To see what will work better for you, start by thinking about the general idea of your plot, how the story will end, where the story will take place, and give some thought to your characters—particularly your main character.

If you're telling your story in the first person and from the main character's point of view, it's important to remember that the main character is telling the story. You're just writing down what he says and does. You're telling *his* story. When you do this, the story will be easier to write.

Select your writing software tool. Any job is easier when you have the right tools. The same is true for writing your novel. You'll need a software writing tool. You may already have MS Word (or the similar free program LibreOffice) on your computer. The three other popular book-writing programs (listed in the order of popularity) are Vellum, Atticus.io, and Scrivener. I like (and use) Atticus.io because it's easy to learn and use. It also allows me to quickly format my book and export versions as eBooks (ePub) and printed books (PDF) ready to submit to Amazon.

Come up with your title. If you don't have one yet, go back and reread Chapter 4. You can change it later if you think of one you like better, but having a title is essential. Don't skip this step.

Hire someone to design the eBook cover for your book. Having a working version of your front cover designed before you start doing much writing is important. Post your book cover at the top of your manuscript so you'll see it every time you sit down to write. It will keep you motivated. Don't be afraid to change your cover as you write your book. You can't have the cover for the print version designed yet because you don't know how many pages your book will have, so you don't know how thick to make the spine.

Now you're ready to start writing—here's how you do it

Start by describing what the main character wants (or wants to happen) and what's standing in his way of getting what he wants. Maybe he wants to get out of jail, or perhaps he wants to get a date with the girl he works with, or you fill in the blank. How you word this information is not important. You'll probably rewrite it later, anyway. It's the facts that matter now, not the words. Start writing and rambling, putting words on the page. Now, you've started writing your novel.

Put a lot of effort into your first chapter

This is the most important chapter in your book, but don't try to make it perfect right now. All you want to do now is set the stage and get things moving. Don't worry about putting a lot of effort into it when you're writing it, but go back and read and tweak the first chapter often while writing your book.

When you start tweaking and perfecting your first chapter, you want to make sure the first part of the chapter hooks the readers and pulls them into the story almost immediately.

As you continue writing your book, review the first chapter, edit it, and rewrite sections occasionally.

When you start writing, don't worry about whether you're doing a good job or not. Let your mind go and write. After all, you may delete what you wrote in the beginning anyway.

Continue telling your story, and write as if you were sitting and talking to one person. Never write like you're speaking to a group.

Follow the steps outlined in this chapter, and you'll never feel confused or overwhelmed when writing your book.

Even if you have only a few hours a week to write, if you follow the steps described in this book, you can write your book and have a copy in your hand in a few months.

The main takeaway from this chapter: If you think you can't write a book, stop and ask yourself if there is any one thing I've discussed in this chapter that you think you can't do. I'm sure the magnitude of the whole process has you overwhelmed rather than any one thing. When you break it into small steps, you can do this.

Chapter 22

How to Publish Your Book

"Start before you're ready."

~ Stephen Pressfield

Note: I lifted this bonus chapter from one of my previous books (with a few updates) to show you how easy it is to publish your book. I hope Amazon doesn't flag this chapter as plagiarism. It is, but I copied my own writing. Let's get started and get your book published. Here's how to make it happen.

Now that you've written your book, you're ready for the fun part—publishing it.

First, you must format your manuscript in two different ways. You must submit a PDF version to Amazon for the printed book and an ePub version for the eBook. Amazon no longer accepts a mobi-formatted version.

Your book's trim size should be 6" by 9". Many writers go with a 5" x 8" trim size, which results in more pages. Doing this would be a mistake for two reasons. The first reason is the book would be more difficult to hold and read. The second reason (and this is even more important) is that the size of the thumbnail image that Amazon shows in their search results depends on the trim size. A 6" by 9" trim size will appear larger than a 5" x 8" book.

Three ways to format your manuscript for Amazon

#1. I use the Atticus.io writing program, and I can download the manuscript in PDF, ePub, or docx format with the click of a button. This program will cost you $145, but you can use it to write your book and then reformat it as many times as you want. Investing in the program is a good option if you plan to write more than one book. I like that the program is easy to use and gives you several templates, so you have a lot of ways to format your book.

#2. If you wrote your book using MS Word or LibreOffice (a free program similar to Word), several videos on YouTube will show you how to format your book using MS Word and how to convert your formatted manuscript to a docx file, a PDF or an ePub file.

#3. As a last resort, several people on Fiverr.com will format your manuscript and send you versions that are ready to submit to Amazon for about $50. I used to do this all the time until I bought the Atticus.io program.

After your book is formatted, you're ready to submit it to Amazon

You can publish your book today using Amazon. It's fast, easy, and free. Your book will be in your hands in a matter of days, and you no longer have to worry about finding an agent or getting a publisher to publish it.

In this chapter, I will show you step-by-step how to publish your eBook and printed book on Amazon.

When you first consider all the steps necessary to publish your book on Amazon, it might seem like a complicated process, but it's not. It's several simple steps. In this chapter, I'll go over them one by one.

Publish your eBook first

Go to kdp.amazon.com, the Kindle Direct Publishing website. If you already have an account, click the "**Sign-in**" button. If not, click the "**Sign-up**" button to set one up.

You'll need to provide Amazon with your banking and tax information. If you're setting up a personal account, they'll need your Social Security number, and if you're setting up a business account, your business tax ID number.

After your account is set up, log in and start submitting information about your book to Amazon.

Start by clicking on the "**Bookshelf**" button and then the yellow "**Create**" button. Next, click on the "**Kindle eBook**" box below the words "**Create a New Title.**"

Be sure you're happy with your title because after your book is published, you can change everything about your book except the title, subtitle, and author's name. These three things can't be changed.

Keep filling in the boxes

After you've entered the title, keep going. Everything else in the process is pretty simple. Keep filling in the boxes.

Here are a few comments about some of the boxes that might be confusing.

The first box asks you to provide a description of your book. If you've already written it, copy and paste it into the box provided by Amazon. If you haven't formatted it, you can use the tools at the top of the box to make some of the text larger and some bold, add bullets, etc. You can type it directly in the description box if you haven't written your description.

It's important to note that your book description should *not* be a description of your book but rather a write-up to convince the reader to buy it.

You don't want your description to be one long paragraph. No one will read it. You need to make the first line bold and larger type, have some bullets, and include several short paragraphs. End your description with a call to action.

The next step is to fill in the seven keyword slots. Enter keyword phrases rather than a single keyword in these boxes. No one searches Amazon for a single word.

Amazon allows you to have 50 characters (and that includes spaces) in each of the seven keyword boxes. Put your most important keyword phrases in the first slots and only one keyword phrase in each slot for your most significant keyword phrases. You can include multiple keyword phrases (up to the 50-character limit) for your last two or three boxes. Don't put a comma between the phrases. When you include more than one keyword phrase in a slot, Amazon doesn't value it as highly as when there's only one phrase, but inserting multiple keyword phrases will get your book indexed for more phrases.

Don't use any keyword phrases you used in your title or subtitle in your keyword boxes. It won't hurt anything, but it's a waste since Amazon will index the words in the title and subtitle.

If you need help finding the best keywords for your book, check out the Publisher Rocket tool. You can use this tool to see your competitor's keywords.

Here is my affiliate link: https://www.aLaptopLife.com/rocket

Check it out and see how you can increase your book sales. It will help you select keywords and the best categories for your book.

Selecting categories

Next is the category section. Selecting the correct categories is crucial if you've written a novel because people often search for fiction books by category instead of keyword phrases.

Selecting the three categories involves a few steps, but they're straightforward. Keep jumping through hoops, and you'll get there.

The instructions in the box make it easy to go through the steps and find the categories where your book would best fit. Be sure to drill down and find the subcategories for your book. Don't list it in a broad category, such as history or boats. You can use the Publisher Rocket program to find the categories that don't have many competitors.

If yours is not a children's book, leave the next section about the age range blank. It doesn't apply to your book.

After you have completed everything on the first page, click the yellow "**Save and Continue**" box at the bottom. This will take you to the next page, which will start by discussing **Digital Rights Management (DRM)**.

I always click on "**No**" for DRM. If you want to learn more details about this, click on "**How is my Kindle eBook affected by DRM?**" Then you can see a detailed explanation. Note that you can't change this after you publish your book. You're making progress. Keep going.

Next, upload your manuscript

For your eBook, you will need to upload your manuscript in ePub format.

If you have included any photos in your manuscript, make sure you compress them in your eBook. Amazon charges you a delivery fee for every eBook you sell based on the file size, and if you have a lot of uncompressed photos, this could add up. When someone is reading an eBook, a compressed and an uncompressed photo looks the same.

Note that later, when you upload the print version of your book, you'll upload it in a PDF format. I'll cover the details later in the chapter. For now, there are a few more things you need to do to finish publishing your eBook.

Your eye-catching cover

The next thing you will do is upload your eBook cover. Upload the cover you have already had someone design for you. Don't click on the yellow "**Launch Cover Creator**" button. If you go that route, you could end up with a lousy cover.

You can change the cover after your book is printed, but take the time to make sure you have an attention-grabbing cover now.

Click on the circle and select "**Upload a cover you already have**." Your eBook cover must be in PDF or TIFF format, not JPEG.

You're making progress. There are a lot of steps, but they're all easy. So, let's keep going.

Next, click "**Launch Previewer**." Amazon converts the files at its own slow pace. This usually takes several minutes, so be patient.

After Amazon has converted the files, take your time and use the previewer to scroll through your book. Be sure every page is the way you want it, and make sure all the links—if you have included any—are clickable. Don't rush the process of thoroughly checking your book. You want it to be right. You can correct any part later, but try your best to get it right the first time.

After checking everything, the next box is where you can enter an ISBN, but since an eBook doesn't require one, leave this box blank.

You're almost finished

Now click the yellow "**Save and Continue**" button to proceed to the last page of the eBook submission process.

Check the box "**Enroll my book in KDP Select**." You can read about it on Amazon and change your selection later, but for now, take my word for it, check this box, and move on.

For territories, select "**All territories**," and for your "Primary Marketplace," select "**Amazon.com**" if you are in the United States.

Now, it's time to set your price. Click on the **70%** circle. To qualify for the 70% commission, you must set your price between $2.99 and $9.99. You might want to set your price at $0.99 or even $0.00 for the first few days as part of your marketing strategy. If you do this, you must click on the 30% circle. (Note: It takes a whole book to discuss book marketing strategies. I cover that in my recent book, *Book Marketing Magic*.)

For the final price of your eBook (after the promotion period), I've found the sweet spot to be $2.99 for novels and $3.99 for nonfiction books, but you can experiment and change your price from time to time to find your most profitable price point.

The book lending option is automatically selected when you select the 70% commission option.

At the bottom of the page, click on the circle that says, "**I am ready to publish my book now.**"

Finally, click the yellow "**Publish Your Kindle eBook**" button.

Congratulations, you've published your eBook

You will see a note at the bottom of the page that says it could take up to 72 hours for your title to be available on Amazon. In my experience, the eBook is usually available in less than 24 hours.

I buy a copy as soon as my eBook is available for purchase. I always read it from beginning to end and click on all the links as a final check to ensure everything is correct. (I sometimes find formatting and other errors.)

Another reason to buy a copy of your book is that Amazon doesn't start ranking a book until there has been at least one sale.

Now publish the print version

Before you submit your print book to Amazon, it must be formatted and saved as a PDF file.

You'll have to select the size of your book and set the margins. The inside and outside margins are usually set differently. Here are the numbers I use when I'm formatting my print books.

All my books are 6" by 9", and I set the inside margins at 0.825 and the outside margins at 0.625. The inside margin needs to be a little wider to accommodate the binding. Play with the margins to see what you like. I set the font size at 12 points.

You can start the submission process after your manuscript is formatted and saved as a PDF file.

It's similar to submitting your eBook. You have to check a lot of boxes and jump through several hoops. Many steps are the same, but a few things will be different from your eBook submission process.

Publishing a printed book is different

The cover you submit will be different. It will need a front cover, back cover, and spine all in one file. If you have hired an experienced book cover designer to design your cover, they will send you the file ready to submit to Amazon.

You must select whether you want your cover to be matt or glossy. I always choose glossy covers because I think they look more professional, but some authors tell me they choose matt for the same reason.

You have to select white or cream paper. I always go with the white paper. I like it better. When you're having someone design your cover, you'll have to tell them whether you will be using white paper or cream paper.

There is a slight difference in the thickness of the paper, which will affect the thickness of the spine. Cream might clash with or complement the colors on your cover.

You have to have an ISBN to sell your book on Amazon. When you get to where Amazon asks you to enter your ISBN, click the box that says, "**Assign me a free KDP ISBN**." Amazon will give you an ISBN at no charge. That's what I suggest you do. The disadvantage of letting Amazon supply your ISBN instead of buying your own is that when Amazon furnishes your ISBN, you can sell your book only on Amazon. I don't sell my books through any other outlet anyway.

To summarize

I always select no-bleed and white paper for the pages instead of cream and glossy paper instead of matt for the cover.

I usually price my print books at $13.95 or $14.95. I've experimented with different prices, but that seems to be the sweet spot. I like to price my print books to earn about $5.00 for each book.

As soon as the book is available for sale, I purchase it at retail price and check it thoroughly. Don't be surprised if you find some errors—I almost always do. Changing the manuscript and resubmitting the corrected book to Amazon in minutes is easy. Pay special attention to the formatting. Make sure your book looks the way you want it to look.

The main takeaway from this chapter: There are a lot of steps involved in publishing a book on Amazon, but none of them are complicated. Keep jumping through the hoops, and you'll get it done. Don't worry about making a mistake. Amazon checks your work and will tell you if you need to change something. You can change almost anything, even after your book is printed.

Chapter 23

How to Market Your Novel

"Whatever course you decide upon, there is always someone to tell you that you are wrong."

~Ralph Waldo Emerson

When you finish writing and editing your book and finally get it published, you may think all the hard work is over. But if you want to sell a lot of books, you still have some hard work to do.

A lot of people write and publish their books, but then nothing happens. No one buys their book. I've seen books that have been published for over a year, and they don't have a single review. That tells me they put zero effort into promoting and marketing their book. You don't want that to happen to your book, so let me show you some simple and effective ways to promote and sell your book.

Put on your marketing hat for a minute, and let's examine what's involved in marketing a book.

Fiction and nonfiction books are marketed differently

People buy nonfiction books to solve a problem, and they buy novels for entertainment. When people have a problem, they often search Amazon for keyword phrases that describe the problem, or the solution.

So, one of the best ways to sell a nonfiction book is to have the keywords and keyword phrases that people will be searching for in the title, subtitle, or one of the seven keyword slots Amazon makes available.

People don't usually search for a novel that way. They may search for a category, genre, or their favorite author, but not so much for keyword phrases.

When promoting your novel, you can't rely as much on people searching Amazon for your book and then buying it as you can when selling a nonfiction book. But since most of the books sold worldwide (both eBooks and printed books) are sold by Amazon, you'll find that Amazon will still play an essential part in marketing your book—especially in getting the initial sales.

How to promote and sell a novel

The best way to market your novel is by asking yourself what convinced you to buy and read the last novel you read. (What about the previous three?) Stop and give this question serious thought. Knowing the answer will help you decide how to market your book.

Did you buy it because you saw an ad? Probably not. You most likely purchased the book because a friend or someone whose opinion you trust recommended it to you. Personal recommendations and endorsements by a friend or someone you trust are a major driving force behind many novel purchases. So, to sell your book, you must get people to recommend your book.

How to get people to recommend your book?

To sell your novel, you need to create buzz, get people talking about it, and get them to recommend it to their friends, but how can you make this happen?

Three things you must do to get people to recommend your book:

1. **First, you have to have a good book.** People will not recommend a so-so book to their friends. They only recommend books they think are top-notch and ones they think their friend will enjoy. Don't waste your time and effort trying to promote your book until it's the best it can be.

2. **Your book has to be memorable.** You want readers to remember and talk about your book for weeks or months. One of the most important ways to help make this happen is for the book to have a satisfying and memorable ending. The purpose of the beginning is to hook the readers and pull them into the story, but the ending is what will have

people talking about your book.

3. **Your book also needs a title that is easy to remember, spell, and pronounce.** People can't recommend your book if they can't remember the title and how to pronounce it. And they can't send emails to their friends recommending your book if they can't spell the title. Also, potential readers can't look the book up on Amazon if they can't spell the title. Don't overlook these points for the sake of having a cute title.

How to get initial sales for your book and get the buzz started

Getting readers to recommend your book to their friends is a proven and effective way to promote it, but how do you get people to read it in the first place? Below are a dozen proven ways to promote your book and get people to read it when it's first published.

1. **Amazon's honeymoon period:** During the first 30 days after a book is published, Amazon will rank your book higher than it deserves to be ranked. They want to see if it will take off. It's essential that you take advantage of this time and do what you can to get as many sales and reviews as possible. Amazon loves winners, and they will heavily promote and market your book for you during these first 30 days.

2. **Get reviews:** Even the best book won't sell if it doesn't have reviews, which are considered social proof.

Why would I want to buy your book if no one else likes it? One of the best ways to get reviews is to make your eBook free for three days on Amazon and then send emails to everybody you have an email address for (even friends you haven't seen since high school) and ask them to "buy" the eBook while it's free, and then leave you a review. Amazon values reviews from verified purchasers way more than from someone who didn't buy the book from Amazon. When someone "buys" your book for zero dollars, Amazon still counts that as a purchase and will show that person's review as being based on a verified purchase.

3. **Promote your book using social media:** I get the best results using Facebook. On the first day your book is free, post a message on Facebook announcing that it is free and asking people to download a copy and post a review. Include a link to your book on Amazon. Post another message on the third day saying this is the last day the book is free. In the messages you post on social media, your emails, and the ads you run, you need to tell the readers the benefits they will receive by reading your book.

Here are more ways to promote your book

- **Select the most profitable categories and keywords:** I use the **Publisher Rocket** tool to find my books' best and most profitable keywords and categories. This program will tell you which categories in your genre have the least competition, how many searches a month a keyword or keyword phrase gets, and how competitive it is. For example, the word "guidebook" gets only 760 searches a month, but break it into two words, and "guide book" gets 4,565 searches a month and is less competitive. Discoveries such as this are what makes this tool so valuable to authors when it comes to marketing their books. Here is my affiliate link to the program.

https://www.ALaptopLife.com/rocket

- **Promote your book to your email list:** Having an email list is one of the best ways to promote and sell your book. Even if you don't have one yet, send a message to everyone you have an email address for.

- **Publish your book using all of the formats available:** Publish your book as a print book, eBook, and Audiobook.

- **Get editorial reviews before and after your book is published:** Ask authors you know for editorial reviews you can post on your Amazon Detail Page. Most authors are willing to do this because you include their book title in their tagline, which promotes their book.

- **Cross-promote with other authors:** In your newsletter, you can announce when another author's book is free or being released, and they will do the same for you. It works even better if the other authors write in your same genre.

- **Run a price promotion through Amazon:** I do this often. When your eBook is enrolled in Amazon's KDP Select program, you can offer your book for free for up to five days every 90 days. You don't make any money from the sales, but you probably don't lose any because the people "buying" your book for zero dollars were probably never going to buy it anyway. But if you can get several of them to post a review for you on Amazon and also recommend the book to their friends, this will be a worthwhile exercise. When you do this, announce on Facebook and your email list that the book is free, and ask them to post an honest review on Amazon.

- **Get interviewed for as many podcasts, blogs, and newsletters as possible:** I've done this many times. It's easy and will continue producing benefits for years. You can do it on a Zoom call and don't even have to leave your home. I've done it both in person and on Zoom.

- **Get an article in your hometown newspaper about you and your book:** Local newspapers love stories about a local author publishing a book.

- **Run ads:** If you're going to run ads to promote your book, run your ads on Amazon. People go to Amazon when they're looking to buy things. They go to Facebook more to surf, connect with people, and kill time. If you're going to spend money on ads, take the time to learn how to do it and track your results carefully. You can waste a lot of money in a hurry, blindly running ads and not tracking the results.

You can't write a book and sit back and wait for the sales to happen

You have to market your book if you want sales. Contrary to what most authors think, even if you had an agent and a publishing company, they would still expect you to do the major part of the promotion of your book.

One other point: You need a book launch team. You need a group of people (3 to 20) who believe in you and your book and will agree to be on your launch team. A small group of friends can be a mighty army. Their job will be (as the name implies) to help you launch your book. They will read your book, post a review on Amazon, post messages on Facebook and other social media platforms they're active on, and recommend your book to their large group of family and friends to get them to buy your book. They will also spread the word about how great your book is. In other words, they will help you get the buzz started about how wonderful your new book is. You have to have a launch team if you're going to have a successful book.

You have to continue promoting your book after the launch

Having a launch team that will do a good job promoting your book will work wonders, but you can't stop promoting your book after the launch phase. You have to continue promoting your book.

You need to continue getting reviews. Amazon values recent reviews way more than older ones, so to keep your book ranked high in Amazon's search results, you have to keep getting reviews. You'll get what's called organic reviews posted by people who buy your book, but you need to help the process along.

Occasionally, you'll need to run price promotions and post information on Facebook and other social media platforms. In your posts, tell people why they should buy your book. Include some of your best reviews and endorsements. You can't publish your book and sit back and hope the sales will continue to come in.

This is one of the longest chapters in the book because it's so important. There's no need to write and publish a book if you're not going to promote it.

The main takeaway from this chapter: If you want to be a successful author, you must know how to market your book. With all the writing software tools, editing tools, and AI available today, writing and publishing a book is easier than ever. The market is flooded with books. The good news for you is that many of the new books being published are low-quality or worse. And what's even more critical for you is that they're not being marketed properly. Write and publish a quality book that you will be proud to put your name on, and then market it the way I've described in this chapter and you will have a successful book.

Chapter 24
Closing Comments

"Our life is frittered away by detail. Simplify, simplify."

~ Henry David Thoreau

You're bound to be serious about writing and publishing your novel or you would have stopped reading this book long before you reached this point.

Until now, it was only a dream, but now you have the knowledge and motivation to make your book a reality.

Think about the feelings you'll experience when you have that book in your hands. Many people dream of writing a book, but sadly, not many will ever do it. They will still be dreaming, and you'll be holding your book.

This book covers many details. Don't expect to remember everything. Use it as your mentor. When working on each part of the process, reread the chapter discussing that topic.

Whether you're writing dialogue, describing a setting, or choosing a title, take the time to reread the chapter about how to do that. Your readers will never know how many times you reread each chapter, but they will know what a great book you've written.

A New York Times article said 81% of people in the US say they want to publish a book. Even though they say they want to write a book, fewer than 1% will do it. Only a few of the 1% who write their book will ever take the next step and publish it.

When you write and publish your book, you will have accomplished what most of the world dreams about. The difference will be that you did it, and they're still dreaming about it.

Your goal is to write and publish a book

Keep in mind that your goal is not to publish a perfect book. Give it your best effort and create a book you'll be proud of, but get it done. You can correct mistakes and republish your new version at any time.

Revising and republishing a book is now super easy. You can change your manuscript, log in to Amazon, and republish the book within 10 minutes. After you make the changes, the next person who orders your eBook or the printed book will receive the revised version. And there's no cost for you to do this.

The world is full of people who are working on a book, and even more, say they want to write a book someday. Most people who haven't started their book will never start writing it, and most who say they're working on a book will never finish it. Maybe they're trying to write and publish a perfect book. Don't let that be you. Many books (even the best-sellers published by the major publishing companies) have mistakes.

Make your book a reality

Don't wait until you're ready and have the time. Start writing your book now, and it will soon become a reality.

Start writing your book today. You're more motivated now than you'll ever be. If you don't take the first steps and start writing your book today, you'll probably never write your book.

Start writing your book right now. I know you're probably thinking you're not ready. You can get started before you're ready. Stop trying to find the perfect time to write your book. There is never a good time to write, and, for sure, there is never the perfect time.

Don't keep the world waiting for your book

Amazon publishes over two million new books every year. But none of the authors have your unique knowledge, writing style, or flair. They can't even come close to writing the book you could write.

Imagine what your friends and family will think about you when you've written and published a book. Almost everyone would like to be an author and have a published book with their name on it, but you will have done it.

Write your first sentence today

Write your first sentence today, and you'll be on your way to having a published book. Don't try to write a profound first sentence—do that later. Today, all you want to do is write that first sentence.

After you do that, could you write a few more sentences? Don't worry if you think what you're writing is not good. It's probably not, and you'll likely delete it later, but your goal for today is not to write something good. Your goal is to start writing.

Basketball players take some practice shots before they start playing, and football quarterbacks throw a few passes before they get in the game. They don't start doing their best work until after they warm up. You need to warm up before you start doing your best work. So, when you sit down to write—start writing. What you write to start with probably won't be as good as what you'll be able to write later. Don't worry about it.

You bought this book to learn how to write and publish a book. Now that you know how to make it happen, get started and write your first sentence today. Even if you don't yet have much of an idea what your book is going to be about, start writing anyway. Just ramble and let the words flow. In other words, take a few practice shots to get warmed up.

One final point: Spend $10 and get a working version of your eBook cover designed even before you do much writing. Doing this will almost guarantee your book will be written and published. I've never seen anyone have a cover designed and not publish their book.

The main takeaway from this chapter: This book has taken the mystery out of the whole process of writing and publishing a novel. Before reading this book, you were unsure if you could make it happen. Now you know you can do it. Don't wait. Start writing your entertaining novel today. You could be holding a copy of your book in your hands in 90 days or so.

Chapter 25
Did You Like This Book?

If you liked this book, do me a huge favor and take a minute to post a review on Amazon.

It would mean the world to me, help other people find the book, and increase my sales. No one wants to buy a book or take the time to read it if not many other people like it.

People look at the number of reviews to see if other people like the book.

I read and appreciate every review.

Here's the easy way to post a review:

Search Amazon for the title of this book. Here it is:

How to Write a Novel and Publish It on Amazon

This will take you to the book's detail page on Amazon. Scroll about halfway down the page until you see the yellow bar graph on the left side. Then click on the box below the graph that says, "Write a customer review." (It's the box the arrow is pointing to in the following screenshot.)

Customer reviews

★★★★★ 5 out of 5

16 global ratings

5 star		100%
4 star		0%
3 star		0%
2 star		0%
1 star		0%

∨ How customer reviews and ratings work

Review this product

Share your thoughts with other customers

Write a customer review

Next, click on the number of stars (five would be a good number), and then go to the box that says, **"Add a written review,"** and type one or two sentences. Then go up to where it says, **"Add a headline,"** add your headline, click on **"Submit,"** and you're all finished. It's that simple.

Posting your review will take less than a minute and mean the world to me.

Writing an Amazon review is not like writing a high school book report. It's not a review of the whole book. It's a comment on one thing you liked about the book, found interesting, or learned from it. That's all you have to say.

It's not so important what the review says—not many people read the reviews anyway—but they look at the total number of reviews. So, the important thing is to post a review.

The main takeaway from this chapter: If you post a review, I'll be eternally grateful—or at least I'll be grateful for a long, long time.

Chapter 26
About the Author

Jerry Minchey is the author of 30 books. He has a bachelor's degree in electrical engineering, an MBA from USC, an OPM degree from Harvard Business School, and he holds five patents.

In his early career, he worked for NASA. He later worked for many years as a computer design engineer before starting his own engineering and marketing company, which he ran for 20+ years.

He has a private pilot license with an instrument rating.

He lives six months out of the year in his motorhome, mainly in the North Carolina Mountains and Florida, and six months in Costa Rica.

His main hobbies are hiking to waterfalls, traveling, and writing. He used to be active in ham radio—KB4LL— but that's not easy to do while living and traveling in a motorhome.

He likes to play bluegrass banjo and old-time fiddle, but playing those hasn't gotten much attention lately. He's also trying to improve his Spanish so he can enjoy more conversations with the locals when he's in Costa Rica.

He is the owner and editor of two websites, **LifeRV.com** and **aLaptopLife.com**.

www.ingramcontent.com/pod-product-compliance
Lightning Source LLC
LaVergne TN
LVHW051635080426
835511LV00016B/2349